P9-DFL-389

IOWA
Off the Beaten Path

IOWA
Off the Beaten Path

by Lori Erickson

A Voyager Book

The
Globe
Pequot
Press

Chester, Connecticut

Copyright © 1990 by Lori Erickson

All rights reserved. No part of this book may be reproduced or transmitted in any form by any means, electronic or mechanical, including photocopying and recording, or by any information storage and retrieval system, except as may be expressly permitted by the 1976 Copyright Act or by the publisher. Requests for permission should be made in writing to The Globe Pequot Press, 138 West Main Street, Chester, Connecticut 06412.

Library of Congress Cataloging–in–Publication Data

Erickson, Lori.
    Iowa: off the beaten path/by Lori Erickson — 1st ed.
        p.   cm.
    "A Voyager Book."
    Includes index.
    ISBN 0–87106–426–X
    1. Iowa—Description and travel—1981—Guide-books. I. Title
F619.3.E75 1990
917.7704'33—dc20   90–38558
                                                      CIP

Cover illustration by M.A. Dube
Text illustrations by Carole Drong
Cover: The American Gothic House, Eldon, Iowa.

Manufactured in the United States of America
First Edition/First Printing

Contents

IOWA

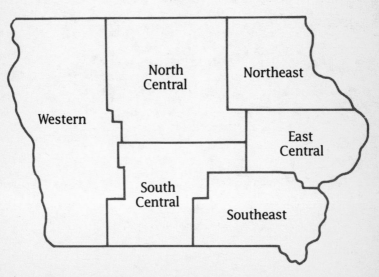

*For Bob, my favorite
traveling companion*

Introduction

In the 1989 movie *Field of Dreams,* there's a scene in which Iowa farmer Ray Kinsella greets a long-dead baseball player who has made a supernatural return to Kinsella's cornfield. Looking around in bewilderment, the player asks, "Is this heaven?"

Kinsella replies, "No, it's Iowa."

The confusion is natural, for I like to think that if there *is* a heaven, it's a little like Iowa—friendly, unpretentious, and full of small towns where the corner cafe serves homemade blueberry pie and strangers are welcomed with a smile. It's a land of soft beauties, of green hills rolling in waves to the horizon, and scenic rivers lined by wooded bluffs. In a world hooked on speed, Iowa rolls along comfortably in second gear. Oh, we can go faster if we have to, but we've found that we enjoy the trip more if we take it at a slower speed.

I've learned a great deal about my home state in researching this book and have come away from it with an increased respect for my fellow Iowans. In one town after another, I met people working to promote their communities and save their local history, devoting countless volunteer hours, and never stopping to think that what they were doing was in the least bit unusual. Most of them are eager to visit and answer questions, and many of these off-the-beaten-path attractions wouldn't exist without their efforts.

In selecting items for this book, I've tried to highlight those that are lesser known and unique. I've also included some that have a wider reputation (Living History Farms in Des Moines, for example), places that should be on everyone's tour of the state. This is by no means intended to be a comprehensive listing of Iowa attractions; there are many more that I didn't have room to include.

A few pointers on using this guidebook: Keep a state map in your glove compartment as you travel, because most of these attractions are off the interstates, and you may find yourself lost without one. I'd also recommend that you call ahead to verify hours and prices. Though all were correct as of press time, they change frequently. Because of their variability, the prices for restaurants are divided into three categories:

Inexpensive—less than $6
Moderate—$6 to $11
Expensive—more than $11

Iowa has more than a dozen welcome centers that are friendly, reliable sources of information about area attractions, events, lodging, and restaurants. Year-round centers are located in Amana, Burlington, Elkader, LeClaire, Bloomfield, Dows, Elk Horn, Emmetsburg, Missouri Valley, and Sioux City. From May through September, welcome centers are open in Victor, Wilton, Clear Lake, Des Moines, Davis City, Sergeant Bluff, and Underwood.

The state of Iowa also publishes an attractive visitors guide and calendar of events. For a free copy, write to the Division of Tourism, Department of Economic Development, 200 East Grand Avenue, Des Moines, 50309; or call (515) 281–3100 or (800) 345–IOWA.

I'd like to thank the many people who helped with the research for this guide, especially the staffs of all the chambers of commerce and tourist information bureaus across the state who gave me materials and tips on the best attractions in their areas. Thanks also to the many friends and fellow travelers who offered suggestions for the book. My husband, Bob, deserves special thanks for being an invaluable help on this project, as he has been on many others.

I hope you'll have fun exploring Iowa with this book. If you're a native of the state, I expect you'll find some places you never knew existed. If you're a new visitor, you have a state full of treasures to explore. You may want to keep in mind, however, the experience of a friend of mine. Years ago he had the task of transporting a native New Yorker from the Des Moines airport to a lecture engagement at Iowa State University in Ames. As they drove out of the city, the bright lights faded away and all that could be seen were the stars and the car's headlights. My friend noticed that the visitor was growing more and more nervous.

"Is it always this dark out here?" he asked.

"At night it is," replied my friend.

"Are you sure it's safe to travel alone like this?"

My friend, a native Iowan, proceeded to weave a story of how it actually *wasn't* very safe to travel at night in the Iowa countryside. Marauding bands of cattle and pigs often attacked vehicles, demanding increased representation from the Minority Human Government in Des Moines. "It's usually best to travel in a caravan of cars after sunset," he concluded with a straight face.

The New Yorker eyed him skeptically, but with a hint of worry on his face. "You're kidding, right?" he asked.

"Iowans never lie," vowed my friend.

So watch out on your travels around the state, both for marauding animals and for locals who won't mind pulling your leg. I think you'll find that your journey will be pleasant. While Iowa may not be heaven, on a sunny day as you travel through its gentle landscape, it's understandable if you confuse the two.

The prices and rates listed in this guidebook were confirmed at press time. We recommend, however, that you call establishments before traveling to obtain current information.

Off the Beaten Path in Northeast Iowa

```
20              16
              Winneshiek
Howard          14
                15
                        Allamakee
              17
              18  19
Chickasaw
                                        13
21                      22          12  11
                                            10
              Fayette              8       9

Bremer                             Clayton

24                      23
                                  7
                                            Dubuque
            25                                        1
              26        Buchanan                    3   2
            27                     Delaware        5  4
                        28                         6
          Black Hawk
```

1. Woodward Riverboat Museum
2. Victorian Progressive Dinner
3. Hancock House
4. Fenelon Place Elevator
5. National Farm Toy Museum
6. Basilica of St. Francis Xavier
7. Wilder Museum
8. Little House in the Woods
9. Cklaytonian Bed and Breakfast Inn
10. Pike's Peak State Park
11. River Junction Trade Company
12. Spook Cave
13. Effigy Mounds National Monument
14. Vesterheim
15. Dayton House
16. Laura Ingalls Wilder Museum
17. Bily Clocks
18. Fort Atkinson State Preserve
19. World's Smallest Church
20. Hayden Prairie
21. Little Brown Church in the Vale
22. Montauk
23. House of Hats
24. Waverly Midwest Horse Sale
25. Ice House Museum
26. Grout Museum of History and Science
27. Star Clipper Dinner Train
28. Cedar Rock

Northeast Iowa

Dubuque County

People who think Iowa is only flat cornfields, feedlots, and barnyards full of hogs should be taken on a tour of Dubuque County. I'd show them the area's steep bluffs, wooded hills, fascinating historic sites, and rich cultural life and then make them guess where they are. Dubuque is the perfect place to begin a tour of Iowa, if for no other reason than to demolish some stereotypes about the state.

Much of what makes Dubuque appealing relates to its long and colorful history as a Mississippi River town. The city is named after Julien Dubuque, a French-Canadian fur trader who received permission in 1788 from the Fox Indians to work the lead mines in the area. The territory was opened to white settlement in 1833, and soon hundreds of new residents—many of them immigrants—were pouring into the new town. The next hundred years saw the decline in mining and the growth of the lumbering, boat-building, shipping, and meat-packing industries. As the city grew rich, its citizens filled its streets with magnificent homes and buildings, structures that stand today as eloquent reminders of the city's past.

One good place to learn more about that history is at the **Woodward Riverboat Museum**. Inside are exhibits on the Indians, explorers, lead miners, and steamboat pilots who worked and lived on this part of the Mississippi. Among its highlights are a recreated lead mine that visitors can walk through and the pilothouse of the riverboat *Aquila*. Next to the museum is the historic side-wheeler *William M. Black,* one of the last of the steam-powered riverboats, now open for tours. The third part of the museum complex is the National Rivers Hall of Fame, a new facility honoring such river heroes as Mark Twain, inventor Robert Fulton, and explorers Lewis and Clark. The three parts combine to make this one of the most complete river museums in the country.

The Woodward Riverboat Museum is located next to the Mississippi at Second and River streets in the Ice Harbor area. From May through October it is open from 10:00 A.M. to 6:30 P.M. daily. From November through April, hours are 10:00 A.M. to 4:00 P.M. (closed Mondays). Admission is $4 for adults and $1 for children. Phone (319) 557–9545 for more information.

Another good way to sample the history of the city—and some delicious food as well—is on a **Victorian Progressive Dinner** held at four of Dubuque's loveliest old mansions. At each stop you'll receive a tour of the house and introduction to its history, plus an elegantly served dinner course. The meal begins with an appetizer at the Mathias Ham House, a home built in the Italian villa style by a man who grew rich off the area's lead mines. Next it's on to the Redstone Inn for soup and French bread, eaten in a wine-colored mansion built by a prominent Dubuque industrialist as a wedding present for his daughter in 1894. The main course is served at the Ryan House, a restaurant that once was the home of "Hog" Ryan, a Civil War general. Your last stop will be for dessert and coffee at the Stout House, built by a lumber baron in 1890 and filled with gleaming, intricately carved woods.

The Victorian Progressive Dinner is available to group tours throughout the year and to individual diners on Friday nights from June through October. Reservations are required, and prices range from $31 to $35. For information, call the Dubuque County Historical Society at (319) 557–9545.

Once you've had a peek at the Redstone Inn and Stout House, you may want to return to stay the night. Both are owned by the Dubuque Historic Improvement Company, a group of local citizens who wanted to save and preserve two of the city's best-loved landmarks. The Redstone is the more fancifully Victorian of the two, with towers, turrets, and cupids frolicking across the ceiling in the front parlor. The Stout House, in contrast, is a massive Richardsonian Romanesque mansion with a more serious, opulent air about it. After passing out of the Stout family, the home was owned for seventy-five years by the Catholic Archdiocese of Dubuque.

The Redstone Inn is located at 504 Bluff Street (319–582–1894). Rates range from $68 to $160 per night. The

3

Stout House is at 1100 Locust Street (319–582–1894). Rates range from $75 to $100 and include breakfast.

Another of my favorite bed-and-breakfasts in Dubuque is the **Hancock House,** a magnificent Queen Anne mansion with a spectacular view of the city. The house is owned by Jim and Julie Gross, who restored the old house to its former glory after it had been allowed to decay for many years. Julie masterminded all the redecorating, while Jim scoured the area for just the right furnishings. "I've driven from here to Chicago just to find the right ends for the towel racks," says Jim. "Sometimes even I think it's crazy being such a perfectionist." Working as a team, the two have brought the house back to life, creating a home that's both cozy and elegantly beautiful.

Hancock House

The Hancock House is located at 1105 Grove Terrace in Dubuque; call (319) 557–8989 for reservations. Six rooms are available to guests, three of which have private baths. Rates range from $50 to $95 and include a full breakfast.

Not far from the Hancock House is one of the city's most unusual attractions, the **Fenelon Place Elevator**. Described as the "world's steepest, shortest railway," the elevator connects downtown Dubuque with the residential neighborhoods on top of a steep bluff. It was built in 1882 by J. K. Graves, a businessman who worked downtown but liked to return home each day for lunch and a nap. The problem was that it took him a good hour to drive his horse and buggy there and back again. To solve the problem, he had built a small cable car modeled after those he had seen on trips to Europe and had it installed on the bluff near his home. Now he could easily fit in both lunch and a nap, and he returned to work each day a happy man.

Then Graves's neighbors started asking permission to use the elevator, and soon it had become a fixture of the city. In the intervening years, the cars and support structure have been rebuilt several times, so even if it *seems* like you're going to tumble to the ground as you're riding it, rest assured that the cars are safe. The elevator is even listed on the National Register of Historic Places—quite an honor for a machine designed to give a businessman time enough for a nap.

The Fenelon Place Elevator is located at 512 Fenelon Place and is open from April 1 through November 30, from 8:00 A.M. to 10:00 P.M. Round-trip rates are $1 for adults and 25 cents for children. (And while you're in the area, browse through the Cable Car Square shopping district at the foot of the elevator, an area of renovated homes and buildings that now house gift shops, antiques stores, and boutiques.)

For evening entertainment in Dubuque, two performance centers in the downtown area offer a variety of shows in elegant settings. The Five Flags Theater was built in 1910 and was modeled after the great music halls of Paris. Today it has undergone a plush restoration that will make you think you've gone back in time a century. A few blocks away is the Grand Opera House, a hundred-year-old stage where Ethel

Barrymore, George M. Cohan, and Sarah Bernhardt once performed. After years of service as a movie house, it is once again home to live community theater. And according to its resident acting company, the venerable old building is haunted—literally—by the spirits of actors who once performed here. "Where else would old actors go once they died?" asks one performer who's heard the ghostly voices. "It seems logical they'd go back to the place they'd loved best."

Regardless of whether ghosts make an appearance during a performance, you're likely to enjoy a show at either one of the stately old theaters. Five Flags Theater is located at Fourth and Main streets and can be reached at (319) 589–4254. The Grand Opera House is at 135 Eighth Street; call (319) 588–4356 for more information.

There are a number of other attractions in the Dubuque area that are well worth a visit, including the Zele Brewery, Old Jail Gallery and Art Center, County Courthouse, Greyhound Park, and several beautiful parks and nature areas. River cruises are another popular way to see the city. For more information on what to see and do in the city, call the Dubuque Convention and Visitors Bureau at (319) 557–9200 or (800) 798–4748.

Before you leave Dubuque County, pay a visit to the small town of Dyersville on Highway 20. One of its attractions is the **National Farm Toy Museum,** a facility housing thousands of rare and antique farm toys as well as newer items, all designed to reflect the agricultural heritage of the nation. There's also a multimedia show describing the lives of farm families from the post–Civil War era to the present.

The National Farm Toy Museum (319–875–2727) is located near the junction of Highways 136 and 20. Hours are 8:00 A.M. to 7:00 P.M. every day. Admission is $2 for adults and free for children.

Dyersville has become known as the "Farm Toy Capital of the World," not only because of the museum but also because of the fact that three of the world's major farm toy manufacturers are located here: The Ertl Company, Scale Models, and Spec-Cast. Each November the town hosts the National Farm Toy Show, an event that attracts thousands of toy collectors and exhibitors. If you can't make it to the show, you can still visit the Ertl Toy Factory at Highways 136 and 20 throughout the year. Guided tours are given Monday through Friday at 10:00 A.M. and 1:00 P.M. There is no charge for tours; call (319) 875–5699 for reservations. There's also an outlet store here that sells factory seconds and overruns.

Another attraction in Dyersville is the **Basilica of St. Francis Xavier,** one of the finest examples of Gothic architecture in the Midwest. The church has a main altar of Italian marble and Mexican onyx, a pulpit of butternut, and twin towers that rise to a height of 212 feet. It was given the title of basilica in 1956 in recognition of its outstanding architecture and spiritual significance and is one of only thirty-six basilicas in the United States.

Visitors are welcome to visit the church at 104 Third Street SW, and information packets are available at the main entrance for self-guided tours. The basilica is open daily from sunrise to sunset.

The baseball diamond made famous in the movie *Field of Dreams* has become another popular attraction in Dyersville. The film tells of an Iowa farmer who plows up his field to build a diamond so that a ghostly baseball team can return to play. The movie was filmed in the Dyersville area, and since then thousands of fans have visited Don Lansing's farm to see the actual diamond. (One couple even came from New York to hold their wedding here.) Don welcomes visitors and promises to keep the field intact as long as people keep coming. The farm is located northeast of Dyersville. Take Highway 136 to the north edge of town, turn right on Third Avenue NE and left on Twelfth Street NE, which becomes Dyersville East Road. Turn right on Lansing Road; the farm is the second one on the left. No admission is charged, but donations for the baseball diamond's maintenance are accepted. Call (319) 875–8404 for more information.

Clayton County

The town of Strawberry Point in southern Clayton County may have only fifteen hundred residents, but it's difficult to miss: A huge strawberry has been erected at the city hall in recognition of the town's namesake. The name was given to the town by soldiers, traders, and railroad workers who enjoyed the bountiful wild strawberries found along the area's trails and hillsides. Each year in June the town holds Strawberry Days, culminating in the serving of free strawberries and ice cream on the last day of the festival.

Strawberry Point is also home to the **Wilder Museum,** best known for its collections of dolls and of Victorian glass, porcelain, lamps, and furniture. Eight hundred heirloom dolls were donated to the museum by two sisters in 1968 and represent a historical overview of doll making from 1700. Everything from a rare eighteenth-century Queen Anne doll to Shirley Temple and Little Orphan Annie dolls are displayed here, along with doll furniture and other memorabilia.

The Victorian collection is a more recent addition, given to the museum by Marcey Alderson, a music teacher and avid antiques collector who had convinced the town to build an addition to the museum in 1985. Though Alderson said that he intended to fill it with items from his collection, the addition sat virtually empty for the next three years. The town was naturally a bit upset, having just spent $60,000 to add to the building. "I have to keep enough to furnish my house," protested Alderson in his defense. "You wouldn't want to leave me with nothing, would you?"

When Alderson died in 1988, the town discovered that the collection was worth waiting for. In fact, the Alderson bequest exceeded their wildest dreams, for packed inside every nook and cranny in his house were eighteenth- and nineteenth-century antiques of exquisite beauty. Today you can see the highlights of Alderson's collection in the museum addition, filled at last. Dresden, Limoges, and Haviland porcelains, glassware of brilliant detail, Victorian lamps dripping with cut glass, and ornate carved furniture all compete for your attention. (A favorite with many visitors is a lamp once used on the set of *Gone With The Wind*.).

The Wilder Museum is located on Highway 3 and is open daily from 10:00 A.M. to 5:00 P.M. from Memorial Day through Labor Day, and on weekends only in May and September. Admission is $2 for adults, 50 cents for junior and senior high students, and 25 cents for elementary students.

For more information, call (319) 933–4920 or (319) 933–4472.

Next follow Highway 13 north to the town of Elkader, named after Abd-el-Kader, a nineteenth-century Algerian chieftain. This small town has nine structures listed on the National Register of Historic Places, a distinction few other towns its size can claim. They range from St. Joseph's Catholic Church to its refurbished Opera House. Also on the register is the Carter House, a Greek Revival home that's open for tours.

Near Elkader is **Little House in the Woods,** a quaint Victorian farmhouse in the middle of wooded, scenic countryside. You can rent the home by the weekend or week and enjoy the trout-stocked rivers, rugged bluffs, and rich pastures that surround it. It's billed as a "farm vacation," a place to learn about farm life as well as enjoy the peacefulness of the country. Located on the thousand-acre Milford Koehn farm, the house is a guest cottage reached by traveling down a winding road about ¼ mile from the main farmhouse. Inside it's furnished with antiques and old-fashioned furniture, plus a huge fireplace downstairs that's wonderfully cozy on cold winter nights.

Little House in the Woods is located about 10 miles northeast of Elkader; call (319) 783–7774 for directions or more information. No meals are provided, but you can do your own cooking in the house's fully equipped kitchen. Rates are $90 for a weekend stay, $175 for a Monday through Friday visit, and $250 for an entire week.

Another unique place to stay in Clayton County is at the **Cklaytonian Bed and Breakfast Inn** in the town of Clayton along the Mississippi River. Its owner is Karilyn Bonomolo, a native of nearby Garnavillo who lived in New York City for eighteen years before returning to her native state in 1981. In 1987 she purchased what used to be the Wilderness Motel along the riverfront in Clayton and spent the next few months completely refurnishing and remodeling it, inside and out.

Today the old motel is hardly recognizable to those who knew it in the old days. The rooms are individually and tastefully decorated with antique furniture, and guests also have the use of a hot tub and comfortable "gathering room."

9

Five of the inn's six rooms enjoy a panoramic view of the Mississippi and surrounding bluffs—and Karilyn even provides complimentary bicycles for those who want to explore the nearby area, plus bottles of wine with the inn's own label and cans of soda from the Garnavillo Bottling Company.

The Cklaytonian Bed and Breakfast Inn (and yes, there is a *k* in *Cklaytonian*) is located on the river in Clayton. Each room rents for $60, which includes a seven-course breakfast (319–964–2776).

North of Clayton is McGregor, a river town that's one of the loveliest in the state. The area is especially popular during the fall, when the wooded bluffs along the Mississippi put on a spectacular color show. At other times of the year, people come here to enjoy fishing and boating on the river, antique hunting in McGregor and the surrounding area, and side trips to a number of historic sites and natural attractions.

One of those spots is **Pike's Peak State Park,** 2 miles southeast of McGregor on Highway 340. Here you can stand on one of the highest points along the entire Mississippi, a 500-foot bluff overlooking the meeting of the Mississippi and Wisconsin rivers. This is also the place where the explorers Marquette and Joliet first set foot on land west of the Mississippi. Nearby are hiking trails and picnic and camping facilities.

In McGregor itself, check out the many antiques and specialty stores on its main street. One store in particular is worth a visit: the **River Junction Trade Company**. The atmosphere inside is like that of an old general store from a century ago, with a tin-plate ceiling, potbellied stove, and counters stacked with bolts of cloth and all kinds of implements and articles of clothing. Its owner is Jim Boeke, a man who has been fascinated by the Old West since he was a boy. When he grew up, he started collecting Western gear and memorabilia but found that there were few sources from which to buy them—so he starting making things himself. Soon he began marketing his work to others, and eventually his business became so successful that he left his corporate job in Des Moines to set up shop in McGregor.

All the items in the store are replicas of nineteenth-century clothing and equipment: Riverboat gambling vests, Abe

Lincoln hats, gunbelts, sunbonnets, Shawnee tomahawks, mackinaws, leather boots, and calico dresses are just a few of the items that fill the store. The company has a thriving mail-order business in addition to its McGregor store and counts among its clients historic sites and museums, performing groups across the country, and even working cowboys in today's West. Jim reports that his overseas business is steadily increasing as well.

River Junction Trade Company is at 312 Main Street in McGregor (319–873–2387). An illustrated catalog is available for $3.50.

Before you leave McGregor, stop by for a meal at the White Springs Night Club on Highway 18 on the west end of town. The atmosphere inside is that of a 1950s roadhouse, and every time I've been there it has always been packed with people—nearly always a sign of a good restaurant. The food is good, standard Iowa fare, and my husband swears they have the best baked catfish he's ever eaten.

White Springs (319–873–9642) is open from noon to 1:00 A.M. Monday through Saturday and from 4:00 to 10:00 P.M. on Sundays. Prices are inexpensive to moderate.

One final attraction in Clayton County is **Spook Cave,** 7 miles west of McGregor near the junction of Highways 52 and 18. Here you can take what's billed as "America's longest underground boat tour." Bring your sweater (the temperature here is an even forty-seven degrees) and take a half-hour guided cruise. The tour is the perfect activity for a hot Iowa summer afternoon.

Spook Cave tours are $4.50 for adults and $2.50 for children. It is open daily from 9:00 A.M. to 6:00 P.M. from Memorial Day through Labor Day and from 9:00 A.M. to 4:00 P.M. in May, September, and October. Call (319) 873–2144 for more information. Camping and swimming are available nearby.

Allamakee County

Beautiful Allamakee County is sometimes called "Little Switzerland," a tribute to its rugged countryside, majestic bluffs, and meandering rivers and backwaters. Here you'll find some of the most scenic countryside in the state, along with some of its best hiking, fishing, and hunting. Although the area makes for poor farmland, for nature lovers it's a delight.

Begin your tour of the county at **Effigy Mounds National Monument** 5 miles north of McGregor. This 1,500-acre area preserves outstanding examples of over 2,000 years of pre-historic Indian mound building. Within its borders are near-ly 200 known burial mounds, 29 of which are in the shape of bears or birds (most of the rest are conical or linear in form). The Great Bear Effigy is one of the most impressive mounds, stretching 70 feet across the shoulders and forelegs, 137 feet long, and over 3 feet high. The mounds are all the more impressive when you realize that their builders didn't have the ability to see the giant shapes from the air but instead worked out all the shapes from the ground level.

The visitor center at the monument has exhibits explain-ing the mounds and the artifacts found within them, plus a film on the culture of the Indians who lived here. Hours are 8:00 A.M. to 7:00 P.M. from Memorial Day through Labor Day and from 8:00 A.M. to 5:00 P.M. the remainder of the year. Guided tours are given during the summer months at 10:30 and 11:30 A.M. and at 1:30 and 3:00 P.M. The tours cover 2 miles of walking and last an hour and a half. Admission is $1 for adults, $3 maximum per car. There is no extra fee for the guided tour (319–873–3491).

Several other parks and recreation areas in Allamakee County are among the finest in the state. The largest is the Yellow River State Forest, a 6,500-acre tract of thick timber, lush valleys, and winding streams. Fish Farm Mounds is a state preserve 6 miles north of Lansing. Like Effigy Mounds, it contains the burial grounds of prehistoric native Americans. In Lansing itself is Mt. Hosmer, a city park with spectacular views of the Mississippi River valley.

Winneshiek County

The county seat of Winneshiek County is Decorah, a pic-turesque community that was the first Norwegian settlement beyond the Mississippi. That heritage is still a source of pride to local residents, many of whom have returned to Norway to trace their families' roots. Throughout the town you'll see evidence of Decorah's ethnic past, from the Norwegian *nisse* (gnomes) peeking out of windows to shops decorated with rosemaling, a type of Norwegian flower painting. Each July the town celebrates its heritage with Nordic Fest, a three-day festival featuring parades, ethnic foods and music, historical displays, arts and crafts demonstrations, and antiques shows.

As a native of Decorah and full-blooded Norwegian, I must admit to growing up with a somewhat skeptical view of the whole proceedings. My friends and I called the summer festival "Nordic Fester" and used to amuse ourselves by wandering the crowded streets talking gibberish in a sing-song voice to make people think we were speaking Norwegian. Today, however, I can't help but admire the immigrants who ventured from the old country to make a new life in Iowa. Even though they did afflict their descendants with such culinary abominations as *lutefisk* (cod soaked in lye), they also left a rich heritage that's well worth celebrating.

To learn more about Decorah's past, visit **Vesterheim,** a local museum that tells the story of Norwegian immigrants from their lives in Norway to their assimilation as Americans. The name means "home in the west," and throughout the facility you'll see the clothes, tools, household objects, and everyday items used by the immigrants, as well as replicas of homes and displays on the arduous sea crossing the settlers endured. There are also many examples of Norwegian folk crafts on display, plus a gallery of paintings by Norwegian-American artists. This is considered one of the best ethnic museums in the country, so plan to spend several hours touring the entire complex.

Vesterheim is located at 502 West Water Street (319 382–9681). From May through October, hours are 9:00 A.M. to 5:00 P.M. daily; from November through April, hours are 10:00 A.M. to 4:00 P.M. daily. Admission is $4 for adults, $3 for senior citizens, $2 for ages 7 to 18, and $10 for a family. Rates are reduced during the winter months.

Next to the museum is the **Dayton House,** a cafe that specializes in Norwegian ethnic foods. In addition to a daily special of an American dish, the Dayton House serves such items as *lapskaus* (Norwegian stew), *rommegrot* (a thickened cream porridge), and *lefse* (a tortilla-like bread made from potatoes). Guests are not subjected, however, to the dreaded *lutefisk*, a dish whose aroma could clear the sinuses of someone ¼ mile away. The Dayton House is open during museum hours, and prices are inexpensive.

Also in Decorah is the Porter House Museum, a Victorian home displaying an impressive collection of rare butterflies, moths, and insects as well as other artifacts from around the world. You may also want to take the time to explore the

Dayton House Norwegian Cafe

area's parks. Dunning's Spring has a waterfall that's one of the most photographed spots in town; Phelps Park overlooks the Upper Iowa River and has a nice network of hiking trails.

North of Decorah on Highway 52 is the town of Burr Oak, site of the **Laura Ingalls Wilder Museum**. This National Historic Register landmark was once home to the author of the famous *Little House* series of children's books. In the fall of 1876, the Ingalls family moved to Burr Oak following disastrous grasshopper plagues in Minnesota. Laura's father managed the hotel that is now the museum, while Laura, her mother, and her sister waited tables, cooked, and cleaned. The Ingalls family lived here for one year before moving back to Walnut Grove, Minnesota.

Local Laura fans borrowed $1,500 to purchase the hotel in 1973 and launched a campaign to raise money for its restoration. With public dances, benefit auctions, book sales, donations, and a "Pennies for Laura" campaign, enough funds were raised to open the old hotel as a museum. Today it's open from May 1 through September 30, Monday through Saturday, from 9:00 A.M. to 5:00 P.M., and Sundays from 10:30 A.M. to 5:30 P.M. Admission is $1.50 for adults, $1.00 for grades 7–12, and 50 cents for K–6. The family rate is $4.00. Call (319) 735–5436 or (319) 735–5916 for more information.

From Burr Oak, travel south on Highway 52 to Decorah, then south on Highway 150 for 8 miles, and then 2 miles west on Highway 325 to the town of Spillville. Spillville is a predominantly Czech community, a fact that drew the Czech composer Antonin Dvořák here in the summer of 1893. Homesick for the companionship of his countrymen after a year's work as director of the New York Conservatory of Music, Dvořák came to Spillville and spent the summer completing his most famous work, the *New World Symphony*.

The building where Dvořák lived that summer is now home to **Bily Clocks,** a museum filled with the hand-carved clocks of brothers Frank and Joseph Bily. The two were local farmers who whiled away long winter days and evenings by carving. In thirty-five years, they created twenty-five intricately carved clocks ranging in height from a few inches to 10 feet, using woods from various foreign countries as well as butternut, maple, walnut, and oak from America. Among the outstanding clocks on display are an apostle clock from which the twelve apostles parade every hour, an American pioneer clock showing important historical events, and a clock built to commemorate Lindbergh's crossing of the Atlantic in 1928.

Bily Clocks is located on Main Street in Spillville and is open from May through October, 8:00 A.M. to 5:30 P.M. daily; in April from 10:00 A.M. to 4:00 P.M. daily; and in March and November on weekends from 10:00 A.M. to 4:00 P.M. Phone (319) 562–5369 or (319) 562–3627 for more information or to arrange a visit during the winter months. Admission is $2.50 for adults and $1.25 for children.

Before you leave Spillville, pay a visit to the lovely St. Wenceslaus Church where Antonin Dvořák played the organ for daily mass during his stay in the village. Then head to the Old World Inn near the Bily Clocks for some coffee and such Czech specialties as *bublanina,* a spongecake with fruit topping.

South of Spillville on Highway 24 is the town of Fort Atkinson, site of the **Fort Atkinson State Preserve**. Here you'll find a partial reconstruction of the only fort in the country built to protect one Indian tribe from another. It was constructed in 1840–42 to keep the Winnebago Indians on Neutral Ground (a 40-mile-wide strip of land established by the Treaty of 1830) and to protect them from the hostile Sioux, Sac, and Fox tribes. The state of Iowa acquired the property in 1921, and reconstruction of the old fort was started in 1958. Part of the original barracks is now a museum housing documents relating to the history of the fort.

A good time to visit Fort Atkinson is during its annual Rendezvous, held on the last full weekend in September. The event draws buckskinners from several states who recreate the days of the frontier. Events include cannon drills, skillet- and tomahawk-throwing contests, anvil shooting, and melodrama performances—and when you get hungry you can sample such frontier treats as venison stew and Indian fried bread.

Fort Atkinson is open from mid-May through mid-October, Friday through Sunday, from 11:00 A.M. to 5:00 P.M. Admission to the fort and its annual Rendezvous is free (319 425–4161).

On a country road near the town of Festina, east of Fort

Atkinson, is the St. Anthony of Padua Chapel, better known as the **World's Smallest Church**. The stone chapel is only 14 by 20 feet and holds four tiny pews. It was constructed to fulfill a vow made by Johann Gaertner's mother, who promised God she would build him a chapel if her soldier son survived Napoleon's Russian campaign. The son did indeed return home unharmed, and the chapel was built of locally quarried stone in 1885. A small, peaceful graveyard filled with old cedar trees is located in back of the little church and includes the grave of Johann Gaertner (who died a natural death, one hopes).

To reach the chapel, follow the signs from Festina. The building is open during daylight hours with no admission charge.

Howard County

One of my favorite spots in all of northeast Iowa is **Hayden Prairie,** a natural prairie 3 miles south of Chester on county road V-26. This 240-acre tract of grassland has been preserved to show what much of Iowa looked like before it was broken by the plow. It is the state's largest remaining section of native prairie. Owned and managed by the state of Iowa, Hayden Prairie contains over a hundred species of wild flowers and attracts a variety of birds and wildlife. The best way to see it is slowly, pausing every few feet to look at the profusion of life growing here.

Also in the area is the Lidtke Mill near Lime Springs, a former wheat mill on the Upper Iowa River. The grounds include the Mill House, which is restored and furnished in the decor of the late Victorian era, and a beautiful park on the opposite bank of the river. The mill is open from 1:00 to 5:00 P.M. Tuesday through Sunday from Memorial Day through Labor Day. Call (319) 566–2808 for more information. Admission is $1.50 for adults and 75 cents for children.

Chickasaw County

While touring Chickasaw County, visit what has become the most famous church in Iowa, the **Little Brown Church**

in the Vale. The church was immortalized in the hymn "The Church in the Wildwood," written by William Pitts in 1857. The story behind the writing of the hymn is part of the charm of a visit to the church. Pitts, a young music teacher, was traveling west from Wisconsin to visit his fiancée, who lived in Fredericksburg. On the way he stopped to take a stroll along the Little Cedar River and came across a place that he thought would make a lovely location for a church. On his return home he sat down to write a hymn describing what he had imagined, a song with a refrain of "Oh, come to the church in the wildwood, Oh, come to the church in the vale."

The years passed, and eventually Pitts returned to the area to teach music at a local academy. He was stunned by what he found, for a small church was being built at the very spot he had visualized in his hymn. On dedication day in 1864, Pitts's vocal class sang the song in public for the first time, and the church and hymn became inseparable. The song later gained wider fame when it became the theme of a popular gospel group that toured the country in the early 1900s.

Today the church is perhaps best known as a wedding chapel. Hundreds of couples come each year to be married in this simple Congregational church—and on the first Sunday in August, many of them return for the chapel's annual Wedding Reunion.

The Little Brown Church is located 2 miles east of Nashua on Highway 346. The church is open from early morning until evening each day of the week. For more information (or to arrange a wedding), call (515) 435–2027.

Adjacent to the Little Brown Church is the Old Bradford Pioneer Village, a reconstruction of what was once a thriving village in the area. The thirteen-building complex includes log cabins, a railroad depot, country school, and the building where William Pitts had his office. Open daily from May 1 to October 31, from 9:00 A.M. to 5:00 P.M. Call (515) 435–2567 for more information.

Fayette County

The crown jewel of Fayette County is **Montauk,** a lovely mansion that was home to Iowa's twelfth governor, William

Larrabee. Larrabee built the Italianate house in 1874 high on a hill overlooking the Turkey River valley, and his wife, Anna, named it after the lighthouse on Long Island that guided her sea-captain father home from his whaling voyages.

The fourteen-room home is built of native limestone and brick molded of native clay and kilned at nearby Clermont, and it's surrounded by forty-six acres of flower gardens and trees. Inside are the home's original furnishings, including Tiffany lamps, Wedgwood china, statues from Italy, onyx tables from Mexico, a large collection of paintings, and thousands of books. The elegant and cultured mansion reflects the character of its owner, a man of boundless energy and ambition, as well as intelligence and charisma. He ran for governor on a platform that called for tighter control of the railroads, women's suffrage, and strict enforcement of Prohibition (his campaign slogan was "a schoolhouse on every hill and no saloons in the valley").

Montauk is located 1 mile north of Clermont on Highway 18. Hours are noon to 5:00 P.M. daily from Memorial Day through October 31. Admission is $1 for adults and 50 cents for senior citizens and children. Call (319) 423–7173 for further information.

In nearby Clermont, you can visit the Union Sunday School, which houses a rare pipe organ donated by William Larrabee, and also the Clermont Museum in the former Clermont State Bank building. On display in the museum are china, crystal, coin, fossil, and seashell collections, as well as antique furnishings and native American artifacts.

One other stop in Fayette should be on your list: the **House of Hats** in the town of Arlington on Highway 187. The museum won a *National Enquirer* contest in 1985 for having the largest single hat collection in the country—more than five thousand of every kind and description. On display are hats from around the country and the world, including handmade hats from Bali, an Amish baby bonnet, and a gondolier's hat.

The House of Hats is located in the Castle House on the corner of Fulton and Depot streets in Arlington. Hours are 1:30 to 4:00 P.M. Thursday through Saturday from June through August. Admission is $2. Call (319) 633–5221 for more information.

19

Bremer County

Twice each year the town of Waverly in Bremer County is the site of one of the state's most fascinating events: the **Waverly Midwest Horse Sale**. The event draws buyers and sellers from all fifty states and every province in Canada, plus overseas visitors from as far away as Australia, Norway, and Japan. With a sale bill that includes over a thousand horses and mules, plus hundreds of harnesses, saddles, wagons, carriages, cutters, surreys, sleighs, and sleds, the sale is the largest event of its kind in the country.

The majority of the horses sold here are draft horses, the massive Percherons, Shires, Belgians, and Clydesdales that once farmed the country. Today they're bought and sold by varied clientele—Amish farmers, lumber companies that use them in areas inaccessible to machines, ranchers who buy them to haul hay, and even places like Disney World that use horses in parades and to pull trolleys. Many of the horses and vehicles sold here command top dollar: A pair of mares can bring $20,000, while a fancy carriage can sell for $10,000 or more.

Even if you're not in the market for a Belgian or Clydesdale, a visit to one of the auctions is an experience not to be missed. The sales are held each year in March and October on the grounds of the Waverly Sales Company on Highway 218 on the northwest side of Waverly. For more information, call (319) 352–3175.

Black Hawk County

The cities of Waterloo and Cedar Falls dominate Black Hawk County and provide a number of attractions that should be part of your Iowa touring. Cedar Falls is best known as the home of the University of Northern Iowa, a school founded in 1876 to fill the need for qualified public school teachers in the state. Today it enrolls about 11,000 students in a wide variety of undergraduate and graduate degree programs. One of the most prominent landmarks on campus is the UNI Campanile, a 100-foot-tall structure built to commemorate the school's fiftieth anniversary. The UNI-

Dome is the other most recognizable landmark on campus. The bubble-topped building houses various sports facilities and also hosts many nonathletic events. For more information on activities at the university, call (319) 273–2761. A campus map and walking-tour guide are available at the Office of Public Information Services, 169 Gilchrist Hall.

Also in Cedar Falls is the **Ice House Museum,** a structure containing artifacts of the ice-cutting industry as well as other historical items. In the days before mechanical refrigeration, natural ice was cut from the Cedar River and stored year-round in this unusual circular building constructed in 1921. Each year, some six to eight thousand tons of ice were stacked within its 100-foot diameter (the circular shape allowed only one wall to touch the stacked blocks rather than two, thus slowing the melting process). In 1934 the ice house owner lost his business, and the structure was used for a variety of purposes in the following years. In 1975 it escaped demolition when a group of local citizens raised money to restore it and open it as a museum. Today you can see the array of equipment once used in ice cutting, plus photographs of the entire process from harvesting to selling. A visit here is certain to make you appreciate your refrigerator and freezer at home.

The Ice House Museum is located at First and Franklin streets in Cedar Falls. Hours are from 2:00 to 4:30 P.M. on Wednesday, Saturday, and Sunday, May 1 through October 31. Call (319) 266–5149 or (319) 277–8817 for more information. Admission is by donation.

Two other museums operated by the Cedar Falls Historical Society are the Victorian House Museum, a historic Civil War–era home, and the 1907 George Wyth House, once the family home of the founder of the Viking Pump Company. The society also preserves a turn-of-the-century country school, moved in 1988 to a location near the Ice House Museum. For more information, call either of the two numbers listed for the Ice House Museum.

In Waterloo, begin your tour of the city with a visit to the Rensselaer Russell House Museum, known as the best example of Italianate architecture in Iowa. The lovely brick structure is one of the oldest homes in the county. It was built by Rensselaer Russell, a Waterloo businessman who completed the house in 1861 at the then princely cost of $6,000. Today it has been restored to its original Victorian splendor and is open to the public for tours.

Open April through October, the Rensselaer Russell House Museum is located at 520 West Third Street (319–233–0262). Admission is $2 for adults and 50 cents for children.

Not far from the Russell House is the **Grout Museum of History and Science** on the corner of West Park Avenue and South Street. Here you can wander through an impressive variety of exhibits describing local history and the natural environment. On the lower level are five full-scale dioramas depicting a log cabin, toolshed, blacksmith shop, carpenter shop, and general store. On the upper level are displays about the geology of Iowa, its first inhabitants, and the plant and animal life of the state. There's also a gallery for changing exhibitions.

A highlight of the museum is its planetarium, where public programs are offered each Saturday at 2:00 P.M. and daily during the summer. The facility features a 17-foot dome and a star projector that dramatically displays the stars, moon, and planets seen in an Iowa night sky. Topics range from the seasonal constellations to the chemical composition of space.

From September through May, the Grout Museum is open Tuesday through Friday, 1:00–4:30 P.M.; June through August, from Tuesday through Friday, 10:00 A.M.–4:30 P.M., and on Saturdays, 1:00–4:00 P.M. all year. Admission is free. Phone (319) 234–6357 for more information.

For a special treat before you leave the city, book a journey on the **Star Clipper Dinner Train**. The ride lasts about three hours and takes you through the scenic Cedar River Valley. Seated at tables set with sparkling crystal, china, and fresh linen, you'll be served a four-course meal prepared by chefs in a specially equipped kitchen car. The entrees include such delicacies as Iowa prime rib, pork medallions, and a seafood medley of shrimp, lobster, and scallops served in a pastry shell with cream sauce—all eaten as you gaze across the slowly passing Iowa countryside. It may not be the Orient Express, but it's one of the state's most memorable dining experiences.

The Star Clipper Dinner Train depot is at Leversee Road in

Waterloo (there's also a depot in the town of Waverly). The cost is $40 per person, plus tax and gratuity. Reservations are required; call (800) 525–4773.

There are a number of fine bed-and-breakfasts in the Cedar Falls–Waterloo area where you can relax and spend the night after a day of touring. Beasley Manor (319–234–2993) is a home built in 1902 in a combination Queen Anne and Colonial revival style. Taylor Manor (319–266–0035) in Cedar Falls is a newer home constructed during the 1940s. The Townsend Place Bed and Breakfast (319–266–9455) occupies an 1880 home built by one of Cedar Falls' most distinguished citizens. Also in Cedar Falls is the Tea Cup Inn, another Victorian-era home (319–232–2260 days, 319–266–2976 evenings).

Buchanan County

In Buchanan County, visit one of the state's most significant works of architecture: **Cedar Rock,** designed by Frank Lloyd Wright and built in 1948–50. The house was commissioned by wealthy businessman Lowell Walter and his wife, Agnes, who later bequeathed their home to the Iowa Conservation Commission and the people of Iowa.

Nearly every item in the Walter house bears the imprint of the famous architect. The overall design is strongly horizontal, lines that Wright felt reflected prairie landforms. The long, low structure is skillfully integrated into the landscape and sits on a limestone bluff overlooking the Wapsipinicon River near the town of Quasqueton. Inside, Wright designed the furniture, selected the carpets and draperies, and even helped pick out the china, silverware, and cooking utensils. In addition to the house, the wooded eleven-acre site has a river pavilion, a fire circle, and an entrance gate that were all designed by Wright. The Walter house is one of the most complete designs Wright had the opportunity to create in a long and productive career.

From Quasqueton, follow the signs to Cedar Rock. The house is open from May 1 through the first weekend in November, from 11:00 A.M. to 5:00 P.M., Tuesday through Sunday. Admission is free. Phone (319) 934–3572 for further details.

Off the Beaten Path in East Central Iowa

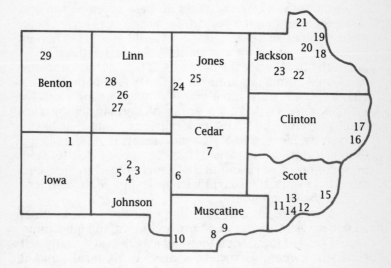

1. Amana Colonies
2. Old Capitol
3. Iowa Hall
4. The Black Angel
5. Plum Grove
6. Herbert Hoover National Historic Site
7. The Victorian House
8. Muscatine Art Center
9. FantaSuite Hotel
10. El Charro Mexican Restaurant
11. Arsenal Island
12. The Children's Museum
13. Vander Veer Park Conservatory and Rose Garden
14. River Oaks Bed and Breakfast
15. River Cruises
16. Clinton Area Showboat Theatre
17. Eagle Point Park and Nature Center
18. Butterfly Garden
19. Potter's Mill Restaurant
20. Mont Rest
21. St. Donatus
22. Costello's Old Mill Gallery
23. Maquoketa Caves
24. Stone City
25. Iowa State Men's Reformatory
26. Czech Village
27. Cafe de Klos
28. Cedar Valley Nature Trail
29. Old Creamery Theatre

East Central Iowa

Iowa County

If I had to name my favorite destination in Iowa, it would undoubtedly be the **Amana Colonies**. Part of the reason is sheer gluttony: The restaurants in these seven picturesque villages are among the best in the state, each serving bounteous portions of hearty German food. If I ever get to heaven, I hope the cafeteria there is staffed by Amana natives.

But the food is not the only reason to visit this community, located 20 miles southwest of Cedar Rapids on Highway 151. Its rich history alone makes it a fascinating stop. The villages were settled by a group of German immigrants, bound together by a common religious belief that has its roots in the Pietist and Mystic movements that flourished in Germany during the early 1700s. The group fled religious persecution in Germany in 1843 and settled in New York State, but eventually sought a larger and more isolated location for their community.

They came to Iowa in 1855 and built their new home on 26,000 acres of timber and farmland in the rolling countryside of eastern Iowa. Soon they had established a nearly self-sufficient communal society, sharing work, meals, and all worldly goods. This system continued until 1932, when the pressures of the modern world and the Depression combined to convince the villagers that changes were needed. A profit-sharing corporation was formed to manage the farmland and businesses, and the community kitchens served their last meal. So ended one of America's longest-lived and most successful experiments in utopian living.

Visit the Amanas today, however, and all around you'll see reminders of the past. These tidy brick villages look more European than midwestern, with their houses clustered in the center and weathered barns on the periphery. For a better understanding of their history, visit the Museum of Amana History in Main Amana, housed in three nineteenth-century buildings set in spacious grounds. There you can view exhibits on the history of Amana, its culture and religious life, and the various crafts and industries of the society. An award-winning slide presentation on Amana history is also available for viewing. The museum is open from April 15 through November 15, Monday through Saturday, 10:00 A.M.–5:00 P.M. and Sunday noon–5:00 P.M. Admission is $2 for adults and $1 for children. Call (319) 622–3567 for more information.

While you're in Main Amana, take the time to stroll through its streets and browse in the many shops filled with the hand-crafted items that have made the Amanas famous. The Amana Furniture Shop sells beautiful walnut, cherry, and oak furniture and has a room devoted entirely to grandfather clocks, which create a delightful cacophony of ticks and chimes. Another popular spot is the Amana Woolen Mill Salesroom, an outlet that carries blankets, sweaters, jackets, mittens, and other items. Free factory tours are given Monday through Friday. Across the road is the Millstream Brewing Company, where premium local beers are brewed. Elsewhere in the village are wineries, gift shops, bakeries, and enough specialty shops to keep you occupied for several hours.

Though Main Amana has the most shops and visitor attractions, don't confine yourself to just one village. A leisurely drive through the countryside will take you on a tour of the other villages, most of which have their own shops, restaurants, wineries, and historical sites. In Middle Amana you'll drive past the villages' most well-known indus-try, Amana Refrigeration. The business was founded by Amana native George Foerstner and is the largest employer in Iowa County.

And before you leave the Amanas, enjoy a meal in one of the village restaurants, known for such German specialties as sauerbraten, Wiener schnitzel, smoked pork chops, and pickled ham. Most serve their meals family style, with over-flowing bowls of salads, potatoes, and vegetables, plus deli-cious homemade pies and desserts. In the words of one Amana native, "If you leave here hungry, it's your own fault."

While I've made a glutton of myself at most of the Amana restaurants, one place I'd recommend in particular is Bill Zuber's Restaurant in Homestead, a cozy spot filled with Amana antiques and baseball memorabilia relating to the major-league career of its founder. Back in the days when the Amanas were still a communal society, organized games like

27

baseball were forbidden by the church elders. Word of young Bill Zuber's athletic abilities eventually spread, however, and one day a scout for the Cleveland Indians showed up and found the seventeen-year-old young man helping with the onion harvest in the kitchen gardens. With no baseball available, the scout selected a large onion and asked Bill if he could hit a nearby barn. The obliging young man promptly threw the onion over the barn roof—and an illustrious baseball career was launched.

After six years in the minors, Bill went on to pitch for ten years in the majors, until his arm was injured in 1948. After returning to his home, Bill and his wife, Connie, established a restaurant in a hotel built in Homestead in 1862. Though Bill died some years ago, the restaurant is still run by the Zuber family. It is open Monday through Saturday, 11:00 A.M.–2:00 P.M. and 4:30–8:00 P.M., and Sundays and holidays, 11:00 A.M.–8:00 P.M. Prices are moderate. Phone (319) 622–3911 for more details.

Two newer attractions in the villages may also strike your fancy. One is the Amana Colonies Nature Trail, located at the junction of Highways 151 and 6 near Homestead. The 3.2-mile trail winds through hardwoods and along the Iowa River and reaches its turnaround point on a scenic bluff overlooking an Indian dam built some 250 years ago.

The recently opened Amana Golf Course is set in 300 acres of forest and has been named by *Golf Digest* as one of the top new courses in the country. Care has been taken to preserve the natural features of the land, and each hole is unique. For information, call (319) 396–9400.

The Amana Colonies Visitors Center, located between Main Amana and Middle Amana, will give you a complete listing of attractions in the area as well as hotel accommodations. The center also has an informational video presentation on the Amanas and a gift shop of Iowa-made products. It is open 10:00 A.M.–5:00 P.M. Monday through Saturday. Phone (319) 622–6262 or (800) 245–5465 for more information.

Johnson County

Johnson County is dominated by Iowa City and the University of Iowa, home to some 27,000 students and the beloved

Iowa Hawkeye sports teams. Most Iowans have at one time or another attended a Hawkeye football or basketball game or else visited the other major draw in Iowa City: the University of Iowa Hospitals and Clinics, where over a half-million patients are seen each year. Thanks to the hospital complex, Iowa City has the highest concentration of physicians per capita of any place in the country—which means that Iowa City is a great place to get sick.

But there are other, more enjoyable, things to do in this tranquil college town. Aside from the Saturdays when the football team has a home game, the pace here is as relaxed as the leisurely current of the Iowa River, which flows through the center of town. The university sits in the heart of Iowa City and is the focus of much of its life, but stroll just a few blocks from downtown and you'll find yourself on tree-lined, peaceful residential streets. One neighborhood you shouldn't miss is Summit Street, a stately parade of Victorian homes and beautifully kept lawns about ¼ mile from downtown.

Iowa City's nickname is "the Athens of the Midwest," and though the title may seem a bit exalted, there are an extraordinary number of cultural attractions here for a town of its size. Hancher Auditorium presents visiting artists and touring Broadway shows; the Museum of Art showcases a fine collection of American, European, and African art; Riverside Theatre (Iowa City's very own professional company) and the University Theatres present stimulating productions year-round; and the university's famed Writers' Workshop draws the nation's top literary talent for readings that are open to the public. Check the university's *Daily Iowan* newspaper for arts and entertainment information, or stop by the Campus Information Center on the first floor of the Iowa Memorial Union.

The best way to see the University of Iowa is to take a stroll along the river walk that runs through its center. If you're an animal lover, be sure to bring along some bread crumbs, for you're likely to encounter the determined ducks that waddle down the sidewalks here with all the swagger of frontier cowboys. Frequent feedings have made them bold and sassy, and their raucous conversations are a steady accompaniment to the bustle of university life.

Just up the hill from the river is the **Old Capitol,** a lovingly restored Greek Revival structure that served as the state's
first capitol from 1842 until 1857. Its golden dome can be
seen throughout Iowa City, and thus if you're given directions by local residents they're likely to begin, "From the Old
Capitol it's about . . ."

Designed by John Francis Rague, the building served as
the first permanent seat of Iowa's territorial and state gov-
ernments until 1857, when the capital was moved to Des
Moines. For the next 113 years the building was used for
various university purposes, until a restoration effort was
begun in 1970. Today the centerpiece of the Old Capitol is a
magnificent self-supporting spiral staircase that leads to the
restored legislative chambers upstairs. This National
Historic Landmark (319–335–0548) is open Monday through
Saturday from 10:00 A.M. to 3:00 P.M. and Sundays from noon
to 4:00 P.M. Admission and guided tours are free.

Next door to the Old Capitol is the venerable Macbride
Hall, home for many years to the university's natural history
collections. In 1985 **Iowa Hall,** its new gallery, was opened,
offering a comprehensive look at Iowa's geology, archaeolo-
gy, and ecology. As you move through the gallery's three
interrelated exhibits, you'll witness the passage of five bil-
lion years. One of the most impressive exhibits is a diorama
depicting the arrival of Europeans into the state in 1673,
seen from the perspective of two Ioway Indians looking out
over the Mississippi River from tall bluffs on the Iowa shore.
Another highlight is a life-sized recreation of a giant ground
sloth, a sight that never fails to draw a gasp from young
children. The museum's lobby features a small gift shop,
plus displays on the pioneering work of Iowa's early natural-
ists. Iowa Hall is open Monday through Saturday from 9:30
A.M. to 4:30 P.M. and Sundays from 12:30 to 4:30 P.M. Free
admission. Phone (319) 335–0480 for more details.

Though the University of Iowa tends to overshadow the
rest of Iowa City, there are other attractions to explore here.
The walking mall downtown is the perfect place to people-
watch, and during the summer months various food
vendors peddle their wares. Another place to get a good,
inexpensive meal on the mall is Bushnell's Turtle, a restaurant filled with beautiful wood furniture and dominated by a

massive oak bar. The sandwiches here are excellent, though you should also save room for the French silk pie (in my opinion, the best in the state). Bushnell's is located at 127 East College Street and is open from 11:00 A.M. to 6:00 P.M. Monday through Saturday (319-351-5536).

If you're interested in folklore, something you must see before you leave Iowa City is the state's most famous grave marker, **The Black Angel**. Located in Oakland Cemetery (the entrance is at the intersection of Brown and Dodge streets), the Angel is a 9-foot-tall, black statue with outspread wings and a menacing air. Dozens of legends cling to the marker: One of the most popular says that a grieving husband spent his savings to place a white angel over the grave of his wife, only to have it turn black overnight because of her unrevealed infidelity to him. Another cheery story says that anyone who touches the angel will die within the year. There's a happier bit of folklore associated with it as well—college students say that you're not a true University of Iowa coed until you've been kissed in the shadow of its wings.

The real story behind the angel is a bit more prosaic, though it has its share of intrigue as well. The statue was commissioned in 1911 by a Bohemian immigrant named Teresa Feldevert for the graves of her son and second husband. When the statue arrived in Iowa City, however, Teresa refused to pay for it, saying that it wasn't what she had ordered. The dispute ended up in court, and the woman was ordered to pay the Chicago sculptor $5,000. The disgruntled Teresa decided to have the statue erected in spite of her dislike of it—and ever since it's been a source of fascination for Iowa City residents.

Plum Grove, at 1030 Carroll Street, isn't as mysterious as the Black Angel, but it's still worth a visit. The mansion was once the home of Robert Lucas, Iowa's first territorial governor from 1838 until 1841. Called Plum Grove after a thicket of plum trees on the property, the home was a showplace in frontier Iowa. In the late 1930s the state of Iowa agreed to purchase it, thanks to a local preservation effort led by a grandson of Lucas. Today it's fully restored and furnished with period antiques. The mansion is open mid-April through mid-October, Wednesday through Sunday, 1:00–4:30 P.M., and admission is free. Phone (319) 337-6846 for more details.

Next to Iowa City is Coralville, a town that has always been a bit overshadowed by its larger neighbor. Named after coral formations left behind from a sea that covered the area 380 million years ago, Coralville today is home to 8,000 people, many of whom work or study in Iowa City. One historical fact may be of interest: Seven Mormon handcart expeditions used the Coralville area as a departure point on their journey west in the 1850s. Informational markers near the university's married student housing complex west of Mormon Trek Road tell the story of these hardy pioneers.

From Coralville, continue driving west on Highway 6 for 8 miles and you'll find Kent Park, a beautiful thousand-acre recreation area operated by Johnson County. The lake in its center is circled with huge willows and looks as though it belongs in an English landscape painting. This is the best place in the county to watch the sunset, and the park also has a small swimming beach, camping facilities, hiking trails, and secluded picnic shelters overlooking the lake. (Another popular recreation spot is the Coralville Reservoir, located 5 miles north of town on Dubuque Street.)

Cedar County

Just off Interstate 80 in western Cedar County is the historic small town of West Branch, birthplace of President Herbert Hoover and the location of the **Herbert Hoover National Historic Site**. Here you'll find his official presidential library, a museum detailing his life, the cottage where he was born, a blacksmith shop, an 1853 schoolhouse, and the Quaker meetinghouse where the devout Hoover family attended services. All are set in expansive, beautifully kept grounds, making this a favorite picnic spot for many visitors.

If you're like me, the thought of visiting the Hoover site might not fill you with excitement. My only memory of Hoover before I visited was a vague knowledge of "Hooverville" shanty towns and the grim man who plunged the country into the Great Depression. After I spent a fascinating afternoon in West Branch, however, I came away surprised and impressed. The much-maligned Hoover, I learned, was a complex man of extraordinary abilities.

Tour the library-museum and you'll learn the history of his life: The son of an Iowa blacksmith, Hoover was orphaned at the age of ten and went on to become a noted mining engineer and businessman. He made his entry into public life during World War I as the director of food relief programs that fed an estimated 318 million victims of war and drought in Europe and the Soviet Union (take special note of the display of embroidered flour sacks sent to Hoover by grateful children). Later he became secretary of commerce and in 1928 was elected the thirty-first president of the United States—a position for which he refused to accept a salary. Defeated for reelection during the depths of the Depression, the indomitable Hoover continued his work as an active public servant until his death at age ninety. By the end of his life he had once again regained the respect of his fellow citizens, and his passing was marked by tributes from around the country and the world.

Be sure to visit the various buildings on the Hoover site, and don't miss the large statue near the library that was given to Hoover as a gift from the people of Belgium. The figure is of a larger-than-life woman wearing a veil, a depiction of the Egyptian goddess Isis. Her air of mystery is irresistible.

The Hoover Library-Museum complex is open from 9:00 A.M. to 5:00 P.M. daily, and admission is $1 for adults. Call (319) 643–5301 for more information.

Before you leave West Branch, take the time to tour its downtown, an area that has been named a National Historic District. A number of antiques and crafts shops line its main street.

Continue east on Interstate 80 for 13 miles and then head north on Highway 38, and you'll come to the town of Tipton, home of the **Victorian House** bed-and-breakfast. This four-story Queen Anne mansion opened in 1984 as one of the state's first bed-and-breakfast establishments and offers five guest rooms furnished with lovely antiques.

The present owners of the home are Lowell and Delores Salser from California, a couple who say that their decision to buy the home was triggered by seeing the Iowa-filmed movie *Field of Dreams*. Before that it was owned by Christine and Robert Gelms, who bought the place when it was in danger of being torn down. Christine had grown up next door to the house and remembers visiting its eccentric owner. The little girl was one of the few people allowed inside, and after she bought the place, she tried to restore it to the way she remembered it from years before.

As in many old mansions, the details here are a delight: stained glass in all the windows, marble fireplaces, Victorian light fixtures, richly carved wood moldings, and intricate frescoes on the ceilings of the living room and library. Most of the house's sixteen rooms are furnished with period antiques.

The Victorian House of Tipton is located at 508 East Fourth Street (319–886–2633). The price is $55 per night for two people, which includes a full breakfast.

While you're in Tipton, stop by the public library downtown and you can see a display of original paintings and lithographs by Grant Wood, the Iowa-born artist best known for his *American Gothic* portrayal of a farmer and his wife. These are museum-quality works, on display in the library free of charge. The library is open Monday through Thursday, 10:00 A.M.–8:00 P.M., and Friday and Saturday, 10:00 A.M.–5:00 P.M.

Muscatine County

Life in the town of Muscatine in the southern part of this county has always been dominated by the Mississippi River. In 1835 an influx of settlers came to the area, and two years later James Casey started a trading post here to service the flourishing riverboat industry. Soon people began calling the area "Casey's Wood Pile"—though by 1850 the growing town had adopted the more elegant name of Muscatine. The word was taken (depending on who you believe) either from the Mascoutin Indians who lived here or from an Indian word meaning "burning island." (It's interesting, however, to speculate on what the town's sports teams would have been called had the original name been kept. Casey's Wood Pile Termites, perhaps?)

You can find out more about Muscatine's history at the **Muscatine Art Center,** a combination museum and art gallery located at 1314 Mulberry Avenue. The museum is housed in a 1908 mansion donated to the city by the Laura Musser family. The first floor is furnished in the fashion of the Edwardian era, and upstairs is gallery space for various exhibits and an art library. In the Muscatine History Gallery, check out the displays on the beautiful pearl buttons that were at one time the city's leading industry. Freshwater mussels were once plentiful here, and the buttons made from them have a sheen that can't compare to the plastic ones of today.

Connected to the elegant mansion is a modern three-level facility with gallery space for the art center's collections. Outside is a small but nicely landscaped area featuring a Japanese garden and native Iowa wild flowers.

The Muscatine Art Center is open Tuesday through Friday, 11:00 A.M.–5:00 P.M.; Thursday evenings, 7:00–9:00 P.M.; and Saturday and Sunday, 1:00–5:00 P.M. Call (319) 263–8282 for more details. Admission is free.

Once you've enriched your mind at the art center, exercise your imagination at Muscatine's **FantaSuite Hotel** on Highway 61. The idea may seem a bit juvenile at first, but the "fantasy suites" contained within are a great opportunity to get completely away—to ancient Rome, for example, or Sherwood Forest. Each of the hotel's twelve suites is decorated in a different theme, and each comes with a spacious whirlpool spa. My personal favorite: Caesar's Court, a room with pink marble columns and a whirlpool big enough for a small dinner party.

For truly rabid Iowa Hawkeye fans, the nearby Tailgate Suite is decorated in the team's colors of black and gold and is filled with Hawkeye sports memorabilia. There are even a couple of lawn chairs on the lower level to make you feel like you're at a tailgate party.

FantaSuite Cantebury Hotel is located at 2402 Park Avenue, Highway 61 (319–264–3337). Weekend rates for the fantasy suites are $149 per night; Sunday through Thursday, $119. Standard hotel rooms are also available.

If you visit Muscatine during the summer months, don't leave without buying one of the region's renowned melons. I've yet to taste any watermelons or cantaloupes that can compare to those grown here. Open-air markets are held on Muscatine Island from mid-July through October.

One other spot in Muscatine County that should be on your list is **El Charro Mexican Restaurant**. This place is truly off the beaten path, but that hasn't stopped it from becoming legendary for its delicious, inexpensive Mexican food. Located in the tiny town of Conesville on Highway 70, El Charro's decor could best be described as "low budget": bare walls, cement floors, chairs that don't match, and lights you could do surgery by. The regulars here consider the air-plane-hangar ambience to be part of El Charro's charm—that and the delicious meals you can get for under $5. (Expect a wait on weekends, though, especially when there's a home football game in Iowa City.)

You might not expect to find authentic Mexican food in the middle of Iowa, but the eight-member Villagrana family, which runs the restaurant, ensures both its quality and authenticity. Refugio came to this country in 1962 and has been operating the restaurant since 1979. Asked what his secret to success is, he proudly replies that he doesn't believe in advertising. According to Refugio, "If you don't like it here, no amount of advertising will make you come back." His system works: Word of mouth brings him all the business El Charro can handle.

El Charro Mexican Restaurant is on Highway 70 in Cones-ville (319–725–4202). Lunch is served from 11:00 A.M. to 1:30 P.M.; dinner, from 5:00 to 9:00 P.M. Tuesday through Thursday and 5:00 to 10:00 P.M. Friday and Saturday.

Scott County

Scott County is home to one of the largest metropolitan areas in Iowa, the Quad Cities. The name is misleading, for there are five cities that come together here on the Missis-sippi: Davenport and Bettendorf line the Iowa side, while Rock Island, Moline, and East Moline hug the Illinois bank.

The first thing to realize is that these are river towns, with a rich history that stretches back some two hundred years. The area was a trading center for the American Fur Company and a battleground during the War of 1812. Davenport was the first city in Iowa to have railroad service, and it was here that the first train crossed the Mississippi in

1856. (The railroad bridge was later the cause of a historic lawsuit between the river trade and the railroad. Successfully defending the railroad interests was a young Illinois lawyer who would later make quite a name for himself—Abraham Lincoln.) During the Civil War, a prison camp for Confederate soldiers was located in the area, and nearly 2,000 Southern soldiers are buried here far from their homes. In the years following the war, the area became a major port for river travel between New Orleans and St. Paul.

Arsenal Island, the largest island in the upper Mississippi, is an excellent place to learn more about the history and military importance of the Quad Cities. The arsenal was established by the U.S. Army in 1862 and continues to manufacture weapons parts and military equipment. With 10,000 civilian and military workers, the Rock Island Arsenal is the area's largest employer.

There are a number of attractions here worth a visit. The Rock Island Arsenal Museum is the second oldest U.S. Army museum after West Point and contains one of the largest military arms collections in the nation. The building is open daily from 10:00 A.M. to 4:00 P.M., and admission is free (309–782–5021). Also of historical interest on the island are the Confederate Cemetery and the Colonel Davenport House, built in 1834.

The Mississippi River Visitors Center is located at the west end of the island at Lock & Dam #15 and offers a bird's-eye view of the workings of the dam, plus interpretive displays on river navigation and the work of the U.S. Army Corps of Engineers. The Channel Project was developed in the 1930s to maintain at least a 9-foot depth in the Mississippi River channel. The result is an "aquatic staircase" created by twenty-six locks and dams on the river. The visitors center is open daily from 9:00 A.M. to 9:00 P.M., May through September. Hours vary at other times of the year. Phone (309) 788–6361 for more information.

Arsenal Island lies in the Mississippi River channel between Davenport and Rock Island and can be reached through three entrances, one on the Iowa side and two on the Illinois. For a two-hour historical tram tour of the island, call (309) 764–1952; or call (800) 521–3346 in Illinois, (800) 227–9967 outside Illinois. The tours operate from April 15 through October 31, and reservations are recommended. The cost is $6.00 for adults and $3.50 for children.

For another treat just north of Arsenal Island, visit The Jubilee, a floating island of glass that houses a fine restaurant. As you dine you have a beautiful view of the water, in a relaxed but sophisticated atmosphere. The Jubilee is located at 2801 River Drive in Moline (309–764–3373). Prices are moderate for lunch and moderate to expensive for dinner.

There are a number of other sites in the Quad Cities that should be on your list as well. The Village of East Davenport at 2215 East Twelfth Street is a historic retail area dating back to 1851. Here you'll find nearly sixty unique shops and boutiques, plus an annual Civil War Muster and Mercantile Exposition held each September.

The Davenport Museum of Art is perched on a bluff overlooking the Mississippi, and features nineteenth- and twentieth-century American art, European old masters, Mexican colonial art, and Haitian art, plus an extensive regionalist collection. Call (319) 326–7804 for more information. The Putnam Museum next door has award-winning exhibits in the natural sciences, regional history, and anthropology (319–324–1933).

The Children's Museum in Bettendorf is a fun stop whether or not you have young children in tow. I recommend borrowing one for the day if you don't have one of your own; watching kids explore the exhibits within is as much fun as looking at them yourself. The museum is housed in an old elementary school building and features exhibits designed with curious young children in mind. While most museums say, "Don't Touch," this one says, "Please Do!" During your visit you can go down a rabbit hole, film your own television show, visit an old-fashioned farm kitchen from 1915, and blow an astonishing assortment of bubbles in a special waterproof exhibit in the basement.

The Children's Museum can be found at 533 Sixteenth Street in Bettendorf (319–344–4106). Hours are Tuesday through Saturday 10:00 A.M.–4:30 P.M. and Sunday 1:00–4:30 P.M. Admission is by donation.

Vander Veer Park Conservatory and Rose Garden in Davenport is a peaceful place to recover from all your sightseeing. The Rose Garden is considered one of the finest in the Midwest, with 1,800 roses representing nearly 145 varieties. The peak blooming period normally begins in early June and continues through the summer. The recently enlarged conservatory presents five special floral displays throughout the year, and at any time it's a lush and quiet place to wander through and enjoy.

Thanks to the recent expansion, the public is also welcome to wander through the greenhouse area that supplies the conservatory. "Most places won't allow visitors to see the back areas, but we think it's interesting for people to see all the plants as they're being grown," says conservatory horticulturist Richard Wells. "That way they appreciate all the work that goes into the displays."

Vander Veer Park Conservatory is located at 214 West Central Park in Davenport (319–326–7818). Hours are 10:00 A.M.–4:00 P.M. daily. Admission is free.

Looking for a place to stay during your trip to the Quad Cities? Try **River Oaks Bed and Breakfast,** an 1850s mansion with a lovely view of the Mississippi River. The five guest bedrooms here range in price from $45 to $60 and come with a full breakfast. Each has been tastefully decorated and furnished with antiques. And for a special treat, take your coffee out to the ornate gazebo near the front of the house to enjoy the view.

The owners are Bill and Suzanne Pohl and Ron and Mary Jo Pohl, two brothers and their spouses who have always loved big old houses. "There has to be a reason for living in a place this big once your kids are grown," says Mary Jo Pohl with a smile. "Running a bed-and-breakfast seemed like the perfect answer."

River Oaks Bed and Breakfast is at 1234 East River Drive in Davenport. Call (319) 326–2629 for reservations.

For more information about attractions in the Quad Cities, contact the Davenport Convention and Visitors Bureau at (319) 322–5142 or (800) 747–7025.

Before you leave Scott County, travel north on Highway 67 from the Quad Cities until you reach the little town of LeClaire. Founded in 1833, this river town was once a boat-building center and home to many steamboat captains, who used to hire on with riverboats traveling past the treacherous rapids near the Quad Cities. Today it's a pleasant town of

3,000 people who take great pride in LeClaire's history and historic homes and buildings.

The town's most famous son is "Buffalo Bill" Cody, who was born on a farm near LeClaire in 1846. Cody became a pony express rider at the age of fourteen and later gained fame as a buffalo hunter who supplied meat for the workers building the railroad lines. In 1872 he began his long career as a showman, taking his Wild West Show to all parts of the United States and Europe.

There are two sites to visit in the LeClaire area if you're interested in the life of this colorful man. The Buffalo Bill Cody Homestead is located about 10 miles northwest of LeClaire near the town of McCausland. The site is open from 9:00 A.M. to 6:00 P.M. daily from April 1 to October 31 (319–225–2981).

In LeClaire, visit the Buffalo Bill Museum on the bank of the river next to the dry-docked stern-wheeler *Lone Star.* Along with memorabilia relating to Cody's life, the museum also has exhibits on Indians, early pioneers, and the history of LeClaire. The museum is located at 201 Riverdrive and is open from 9:00 A.M. to 5:00 P.M. daily May 15 through October 15. Winter hours are 9:00 A.M. to 5:00 P.M. on Saturday and Sunday. Phone (319) 289–5580.

To explore the mighty Mississippi firsthand, board a riverboat at LeClaire for a cruise on one of the prettiest sections of the river. **River Cruises** operates two boats and offers two-day trips on the river, with overnight accommodations in Galena, Illinois. The *Julia Belle Swain* is one of only five authentic river steamboats remaining in the United States. (The boat is so authentic, in fact, that is has been used in several movie adaptations of Mark Twain's works.) Her sister ship, the *Twilight,* is a slightly larger and more luxurious boat, decorated in the same Victorian steamboat architecture.

I've taken a number of river cruises up and down the Mississippi, but the ones I took on these two boats were the most enjoyable by far. The food is delicious, the scenery magnificent, the entertainment enjoyable, and the boats themselves exquisite. One of my all-time favorite memories is watching a Technicolor sunset from the pilothouse of the *Julia Belle Swain.*

The *Julia Belle Swain*

River cruises on both boats board at LeClarie in the morning, travel upriver all day, and dock at Galena, where guests stay overnight at Chestnut Mountain Resort. The next day you can tour Galena and then board the boat again at noon for a leisurely trip back to LeClaire. The boats run from the end of May through October, and reservations are required. Tickets are $185 per person (double occupancy), which includes all meals, entertainment, and lodging. In Illinois call (800) 237–1660; outside Illinois call (800) 331–1467. For a free brochure, write to River Cruises, P.O. Box 406, Galena, IL 61036.

Clinton County

Like the Quad Cities, Clinton is a town dominated by the Mississippi River. During the late nineteenth century, Clinton became an important transportation and lumbering center, and today it continues to be an active industrial area.

Clinton takes great pride in its history as a river town, and you can enjoy an echo of that past at the **Clinton Area Showboat Theatre**. This is a theater group that performs each summer aboard the *City of Clinton* showboat—an authentic paddle-wheeler permanently dry-docked on the riverbank in Clinton's Riverview Park. Recalling the days when lavish showboats plied their way up and down the river, the theater is the perfect place to complete a day's touring along the Mississippi.

These aren't amateur productions, either. Each spring the theater recruits nationally to produce its June-through-August summer stock season. Performances are given in a 225-seat air-conditioned theater and include contemporary works as well as old standards. Musicals, comedies, and dramas are offered each season.

The *City of Clinton* showboat is docked at Riverview Park, Sixth Avenue North along the Mississippi. Tickets to the performances range from $7.50 to $8.50; call (319) 243–2231 for more information. The showboat itself is open daily for tours from Memorial Day through Labor Day. Hours are 12:30–6:00 P.M. (319–243–9085).

Travel to the north end of Clinton and you'll find **Eagle Point Park and Nature Center,** a recreation area perched high on a bluff overlooking the river. The park itself contains 200 acres with numerous hiking trails and picnic areas. Be sure to see the 35-foot observation tower built of locally quarried stone that stands on a promontory above the river.

The nature center adjacent to the park will help you appreciate the beauty and ecology of the area. During the summer and early fall, the center manages various animal exhibits and a petting zoo, plus a pond for fish and waterfowl. Nearby is the Flannery School, a restored one-room schoolhouse, and just to the east is a prairie demonstration area with native prairie flowers and grasses. While schoolchildren make up a good part of the nature center's clientele, adults are always welcome as well.

The Eagle Point Park and Nature Center is located on North Third Street on the northern edge of Clinton. Call (319) 243–1260 for more information.

Jackson County

Scenic Jackson County is one of Iowa's largely undiscovered treasures, an area of rolling hills, limestone bluffs, and meandering rivers. This is a "driftless area," meaning that the leveling forces of the Ice Age glaciers passed it by. The result: beautiful scenery and a ruggedness that belies Iowa's flat-as-a-pancake reputation.

Follow Highway 52 along the Mississippi and you can view the best of that beautiful scenery. At Bellevue you'll find one of the river's most charming towns, a place that lives up to its name, which means "beautiful view." Begin your tour at Lock & Dam #12 in the middle of town and then wander through Bellevue's shopping district, an area lined with century-old stone and brick buildings. Many now house stores selling antiques, collectibles, and arts and crafts.

For a treat of a different sort, visit the **Butterfly Garden** at Bellevue State Park. And just what is a butterfly garden, you ask? From a butterfly's point of view, it's heaven. This one-acre garden (one of only a handful in North America) is carefully planned to provide for the care and feeding of nature's most beautiful and delicate creatures. In it are a mixture of plants that range from radishes and carrots to milkweeds and stinging nettles that play host to some sixty species of butterflies that hover here each spring, summer, and fall. Interspersed among the plants are large rocks that make ideal basking spots for butterflies, plus a small pond where they can get water.

This serene oasis is the product of thousands of hours of volunteer labor done by Bellevue citizens, and in particular Judy Pooler, who in 1986 received the Governor's Award for volunteer service to the state of Iowa. Pooler first came across the idea for a butterfly garden in a magazine in 1984 and soon persuaded the park to develop a former meadow into a garden. Since then she has traveled to Newfoundland and South America to study butterflies and has corresponded with lepidopterists around the country in her quest to expand and improve the garden.

Pooler says that the best time to visit the garden is on a sunny day with little wind. The Butterfly Garden is located in Bellevue State Park, ½ mile south of town off Highway 52.

You can refresh yourself after an afternoon of butterfly watching at **Potter's Mill Restaurant,** a six-story mill built in 1843 that now houses a fine dining establishment and gift emporium. During the nineteenth century the mill sold its flour to wholesalers as far away as New York and Boston, but by the time Bellevue native Daryll Eggers bought it in 1980, it had fallen into nearly total disrepair (a family of beavers had even set up housekeeping in a flooded basement room).

During the next five years, Eggers and his wife, Carolyn, along with his brother and sister-in-law, Dan and Caroline Eggers, worked to repair and restore the property. One of their goals was to save as much of the old mill equipment as possible, so that today you can see several millstones and numerous other pieces of machinery on display throughout the restaurant.

Now listed on the National Register of Historic Places, Potter's Mill features a menu of midwestern favorites that includes steak, ham, roast pork loin, shrimp, and prime rib. Prices range from moderate to expensive. Many of the selections are based on Eggers family recipes, and all the breads are baked fresh daily in the restaurant's kitchen.

Potter's Mill is at 300 Potter's Drive in Bellevue. Lunch is served daily from 11:00 A.M. to 2:00 P.M.; dinner, from 5:00 P.M.; and Sunday brunch, from 10:00 A.M. to 2:00 P.M. During the winter months, the restaurant is only open on Friday, Saturday, and Sunday. Call (319) 872–4237 or (800) 397–0248 for reservations.

Another gem of a restoration in Bellevue is **Mont Rest,** a bed-and-breakfast inn built in 1893. Nestled into a wooded hillside overlooking the town and river, Mont Rest is a luxurious inn owned by Christine and Robert Gelms (former owners of the Victorian House in Tipton). Like the Eggers family, they bought their property in a very run-down state but have now restored it to its original elegance (with some modern additions like whirlpool baths).

Five bedrooms are open to guests, each beautifully decorated and furnished with antiques. The most unusual is located in a tower that was once a gambling den for the home's original owner. The bedroom has a panoramic view of the Mississippi and a roof garden right outside its door.

Be forewarned, however: In order to go to the bathroom you have to walk outside and down a steep set of stairs. I think that adds to its charm, though a visitor may think differently on a frigid January night. "The owner wanted to make the room as inaccessible as possible so that he'd have plenty of warning if the place was raided for gambling," explains Christine Gelms.

Mont Rest is located at 300 Spring Street in Bellevue (319–872–4220). Prices for double occupancy range from $50 to $75 a night, with a full country breakfast included.

Travel north on Highway 52 for 10 miles and you'll reach **St. Donatus,** a small village famous for its Old World architecture and traditions. Its settlers were immigrants from Luxembourg who tried to duplicate the architecture, dress, and customs of their native land in their new home. Here they built beautiful homes of limestone quarried from nearby bluffs, buildings that stand as solid today as they did a hundred years ago. St. Donatus has the largest and best collection of Luxembourg nineteenth-century architecture outside of Europe.

One of the village's main attractions is the Outdoor Way of the Cross, the first of its kind in America. Built in 1861, it consists of fourteen brick alcoves scattered along a winding path behind the St. Donatus Catholic Church. Each alcove contains an original lithograph depicting Christ's journey on Good Friday. At the top of the hill is the Pieta Chapel, a replica of a church in Luxembourg.

Other attractions in St. Donatus include Gehlen House and Barn, a house built in 1848 that is listed on the National Register of Historic Places and now houses a doll museum. The museum is open daily from 8:30 A.M. to 5:30 P.M., and admission is $3 for adults. Phone (319) 773–2405 for more information.

A good way to view St. Donatus is to sign up for a group tour and noon luncheon, available at $12 per person. For more information, call (319) 773–2680 or (319) 773–2405.

From St. Donatus, return south on Highway 52 to Bellevue and then take Highway 62 south to Maquoketa. One mile east of town you'll find another mill that's been restored, **Costello's Old Mill Gallery**. The 1867 stone building was bought and restored by nationally known wildlife artist

Patrick J. Costello, who displays and sells both his work and that of other artists. Many days you can find Costello working in his studio at the back of the mill, where visitors are invited to watch him as he sketches. "At times it's distracting," he admits, "but I think it helps people be more appreciative of the work I do."

Costello's Old Mill Gallery is located just east of Maquoketa on Highway 64 (319–652–3351). From January through March the mill is open Wednesday through Sunday from 10:00 A.M. to 6:00 P.M.; from April through December, it's open daily from 10:00 A.M. to 6:00 P.M.

In Maquoketa itself several attractions are worth a visit. The Decker House Inn was built in 1875 and now houses a restaurant and bed-and-breakfast. North of town on Highway 61 is Banowetz Antiques, the Midwest's largest antiques shop, with over two acres of merchandise. And for

Costello's Old Mill Gallery

an introduction to the history of the area, tour the Jackson County Historical Museum on the Jackson County Fairgrounds.

Then take Highway 428 west of town to the **Maquoketa Caves,** one of Iowa's most unusual geologic formations. This 272-acre state park contains a labyrinth of underground caverns and woodland trails. You can reach the thirteen caves scattered throughout the park by well-marked and sometimes rugged trails. While two of the main caves are lighted, flashlights are needed in the others.

Indian pottery, arrowheads, spears, and other artifacts found in the caves provide proof that they were used by native tribes for hundreds of years. When the caves were first discovered by whites before the Civil War, lovely stalactites and stalagmites were found, but unfortunately, souvenir hunters have robbed the caves of most of these. Two monuments that remain are a balanced rock and natural bridge.

Camping and picnic sites are available in the park, and the nearby Sagers Museum is open Memorial Day through Labor Day Saturdays and Sundays, noon–5:00 P.M. The museum contains native American and natural artifacts from the area and is located near the entrance to the park on Highway 428. Call (319) 652–5833 for more information.

Jones County

Tiny **Stone City** in western Jones County has been called the most accurately named town in the state of Iowa. This is indeed a city of stone—dolomite limestone, to be exact, a high-quality building material similar to that found in the part of the Italian Alps known as the Dolomites.

During the mid-nineteenth century this valley was one of the most prosperous areas in the Midwest, the center of a thriving stone-cutting industry that supplied building material to points throughout the country. The workers who labored in the quarries were primarily Irish immigrants, as was John A. Green, the dynamic businessman who was most responsible for the town's growth. In 1883 he built a majestic mansion overlooking the town, furnishing it with the finest amenities. Later a three-story opera house was built to entertain his guests, with a stage that drew such luminaries as Jenny Lind and General Tom Thumb.

The boom days of Stone City, however, came to an abrupt end at the turn of the century with the growing use of cement. As the quarries lay idle, the town's population dwindled to a few dozen people, and the magnificent stone mansions and buildings stood empty. It wasn't until the early 1930s that the town came alive again, when famed Iowa artist Grant Wood chose it as the site for his summer art colony. The Green mansion bustled once again as the headquarters for the school, while instructors and students roamed the hills in search of inspiration. (Wood's idyllic painting *Stone City* shows the little village nestled among rolling hills and fields.)

In the intervening years Stone City has remained a quiet, nearly deserted hamlet, though it's experiencing a kind of renaissance today as area residents work to preserve the buildings and develop visitor attractions. The best time to visit the village is each year on the second Sunday in June, when Stone City hosts the Grant Wood Art Festival. Area artists come to demonstrate and sell their work, tours are offered of the town's historic ruins, and strolling entertainers perform throughout the village. For more information, call (319) 462–4267 or (319) 462–3988.

At any time of year, the Stone City General Store offers fine entertainment in the evenings. This stone structure overlooks the Wapsipinicon River in the center of the village and contains a cozy bar downstairs and a small, intimate performance space upstairs. Folk music concerts are held here each Friday, Saturday, and Sunday, featuring touring national performers as well as local artists. For a schedule, call (319) 462–4719.

To see some of the fruits of the Stone City quarries, travel west 2 miles to the town of Anamosa, site of the **Iowa State Men's Reformatory**. Beginning in 1873, prisoners labored to construct the prison, using stone quarried from the nearby Stone City area. Upon its completion, Iowans dubbed it the "White Palace of the West," a tribute to its imposing architecture, beautiful stone walls, and immaculate landscaping. And while it may seem strange to think of a prison as a tourist attraction, the austere stateliness of the structure makes it one of Iowa's more unusual landmarks.

The prison today looks much the same as it did a hundred years ago, down to the regal stone lions guarding its entrance. During the summer months, a formal garden in front of the prison is filled with blooming flowers. Although visitors are not allowed inside the prison, they are invited to enjoy the outside grounds.

The Iowa State Men's Reformatory is located at 406 North High Street in Anamosa, on the west end of the downtown area.

Linn County

The center of life in Linn County is Cedar Rapids, eastern Iowa's largest city. A number of famous Iowans are associated with Cedar Rapids: Artist Grant Wood made his home here for many years, Mamie Doud Eisenhower lived here as a child, and the famous Cherry Sisters spent most of their lives here. The name doesn't sound familiar? The Cherry Sisters (Effie, Addie, and Jessie) were stage performers at the turn of the century whose act was so bad that it sometimes had to be "presented behind nets to protect the sisters from vegetables, fruit, and other missiles hurled at them," according to one Iowa history book. Nevertheless, their performances were so popular that they enabled the Oscar Hammerstein Theatre in New York to pay off its mortgage in one season. The Cherry Sisters then returned to Cedar Rapids, where they spent the rest of their lives.

Cedar Rapids today has many attractions that don't deserve a single rotten vegetable. One of my favorites is the city's **Czech Village,** a 3-block area of Czech shops and restaurants on Sixteenth Avenue SW. One-third of the population in Cedar Rapids is of Czech origin, making it the dominant ethnic group in the city. The village area is a center for preserving that heritage and is the site of several ethnic festivals and businesses.

Stop by the Sykora Bakery for an authentic taste of Czech culture—one of their specialties is *kolaches,* a fruit-filled pastry. Then wander down to the Czech Museum and Immigrant

Home, a building filled with exhibits detailing Czech culture both in the Old World and the New. Take special note of the elaborate native costumes on display here, each from a different region and community. Other exhibits include a restored Czech immigrant home from the period 1880–1900. The museum also sponsors live demonstrations of such traditional arts and crafts as lace making, feather stripping, and Easter egg painting.

The Czech Museum and Immigrant Home is at 10 Sixteenth Avenue SW (319–362–8500). The museum is open from April 15 through November 15, Tuesday through Friday, 10:00 A.M.–4:00 P.M. and year-round on Saturdays from 9:30 A.M. to 4:300 P.M. A donation of $2.50 is requested.

Also in the Czech Village area are a number of gift shops, plus Polehna's Meat Market, a shop that smokes its own meat and sells various ethnic sausages and meats. And for an authentic Czech meal, visit the Lion's Pride Restaurant, where you can order such treats as *svickova* (marinated fillet of beef with dumpling and cranberry sauce) and *jaternice* (seasoned pork sausage with boiled potatoes and sauerkraut). Prices are moderate to expensive. Lion's Pride Restaurant can be found at 95 Sixteenth Avenue SW; call (319) 362–1216.

Another unusual restaurant in Cedar Rapids is the **Cafe de Klos,** located in an older brick home on the city's southeast side. Its owner, Gary Dvorak, traveled to Holland some years ago and came across a restaurant in Amsterdam with a delicious secret sauce. He persuaded the owner to give him the recipe, and eventually he and his wife, Joan, opened their own restaurant based on the one in Holland.

If you like the sauce, you'll love Cafe de Klos. Nearly everything they serve—ribs, chicken, pork loin, seafood, steak—is flavored with it, including garlic bread and French fries. (While the Dvoraks won't reveal the recipe, the sauce has a definite curry flavor to it.)

Cafe de Klos is located at 821 Third Avenue SE (319–362–9340). Evening dining is from 5:00 to 10:00 P.M., Tuesday through Saturday. On Fridays, the cafe also serves lunch from 11:00 A.M. to 2:00 P.M. Reservations are recommended, and prices are expensive.

Other sites of interest in Cedar Rapids include the

restored Brucemore Mansion, Indian Creek Nature Center, Seminole Valley Farm, and Usher's Ferry Pioneer Village. One of its newest attractions is the Cedar Rapids Museum of Art, a $10 million structure that opened in 1989. The facility houses an outstanding regional collection, including the nation's largest collection of works by Grant Wood and Marvin Cone. For more visitor information on Cedar Rapids, call (319) 398–5009.

Before you leave Linn County, check out the **Cedar Valley Nature Trail,** a 52-mile route that follows a former railroad line between Cedar Rapids and Waterloo. Opened officially in 1984, the trail is the longest one of its kind in Iowa and the longest one in the country connecting two metropolitan areas.

One advantage of the trail is that its grade is never more than 3 percent, making it an easy place to hike, bike, or cross-country ski. The path winds through grasslands, woods, wetlands, and farms, with abundant wildlife along the way, from wild turkeys to white-tailed deer. It also passes through the towns of Gilbertville, La Porte City, Brandon, Urbana, Lafayette, and Center Point, all of which have rest rooms and water available.

To enter the trail from Cedar Rapids, drive north on Interstate 80, take Exit 25, and follow the signs to the trail head. A daily pass of $1 is available at county parks and from local businesses and trail park rangers. Call (319) 398–3505 for more information.

Benton County

About the last place you'd expect to find a professional theater company is Garrison, Iowa, home to some four hundred people. Nevertheless, the **Old Creamery Theatre** has been bringing dramatic delights to Garrison since its founding in 1971. The nonprofit organization was begun by Thomas Johnson and nine theater colleagues from Iowa State University and the University of Iowa, a group determined to bring high-quality live theater to Iowans, particularly those in rural communities. In the years since then they've fulfilled their goal admirably, both at the theater in Garrison and in touring productions around the state. In 1980 the theater was awarded the Iowa Distinguished Service Award, the first time such an award had been presented to an organization.

Visit the Old Creamery Theatre and you can see where the name comes from: The building is a former dairy transformed into a two-story complex housing two stages. Here you can see an eclectic mixture of comedy and drama, at prices far lower than those charged by most professional theaters (ticket prices here are between $10 and $12). Before the performance, enjoy dinner at the Stage Door Restaurant. On Wednesday and Thursday there's a baked fish and chicken special, and on Friday, Saturday, and Sunday there's a full buffet with three meats plus a soup and salad bar. Serving times Wednesday through Saturday are 5:30–7:15 P.M. and Sundays from 4:00 to 6:15 P.M. Prices are moderate. For ticket information or dinner reservations, call (319) 477–3925 or (800) 332–5200.

Off the Beaten Path in Southeast Iowa

Mahaska
15

Keokuk

3 2 1
4

Washington

5
Louisa
6

Monroe
16

Wapello
14 13
12

Jefferson
10
11

Henry
7
8 9

Des Moines

17

Appanoose

Davis

Van Buren
18 19
20

Lee
24

27 26
25

23 22
21

1. Future Birthplace of Captain James T. Kirk
2. Kalona Quilt Show and Sale
3. Kalona Historical Village
4. Heartland Bicycle Tours
5. Columbus Junction Swinging Bridge
6. Toolesboro Indian Mounds
7. Midwest Old Threshers Reunion
8. Museum of Repertoire Americana
9. Goo-Cheez Designer Diner
10. Maharishi International University
11. Great Midwestern Ice Cream Company
12. American Gothic House
13. Chief Wapello's Memorial Park
14. Air Power Museum
15. Nelson Pioneer Farm Museum
16. Albia
17. Rathbun Fish Hatchery
18. Hotel Manning
19. Bentonsport
20. Bonaparte's Retreat
21. *George M. Verity* Riverboat Museum
22. Keokuk Bald Eagle Appreciation Days
23. Liz Clark's
24. Old Fort Madison
25. Snake Alley
26. Burlington Steamboat Days
27. MADRAC

Southeast Iowa

Washington County

If you wish to "boldly go where no man has gone before," the trek begins in tiny Riverside, the **Future Birthplace of Captain James T. Kirk**. In 1985 the Riverside City Council voted unanimously to declare a spot behind what used to be the town's barbershop as the place where Captain Kirk of "Star Trek" fame would one day be born.

Riverside has official proof to back up its claim. Gene Roddenberry's book, *The Making of Star Trek,* says that Kirk "was born in a small town in the State of Iowa." The town contacted Roddenberry and received a certificate confirming its birthplace status, and thus was born one of Iowa's most famous future historical sites.

On the last Saturday in June each summer, Riverside celebrates Kirk's future birthdate in the year 2228 by holding its Trek Fest. This gathering of devout Trekkies includes videos of the show, a swap meet, and fan club meetings, plus such interplanetary diversions as a demolition derby, volleyball tournament, beer tent, and a parade on Main Street. (And for a truly unique gift, at the festival you can purchase a vial of dirt from the official future birthplace.) All proceeds from Trek Fest go to community projects and for constructing a permanent monument to mark Kirk's birth. In the meantime, the town marks its advance status with a 20-foot replica of the *Enterprise* on display in a downtown park. Captain Kirk would undoubtedly be proud. For more information about Trek Fest, write to the Riverside Area Community Club, Box 55, Riverside, 52327.

To journey from the future to the past, simply drive 6 miles west from Riverside on Highway 22 to Kalona, home of the largest Amish-Mennonite community west of the Mississippi River. Seven Amish congregations (with about seven hundred members) are in the area, along with seventeen Mennonite churches. Buggies travel the highway's shoulders here right beside more modern vehicles, and as you drive through the countryside you're likely to see Amish farmers working their fields with horse-drawn equipment.

Downtown Kalona has a wide selection of antiques, bakery goods, and locally made gifts and craft items, including the hand-stitched quilts for which the area is famous. In April the town hosts its annual **Kalona Quilt Show and Sale,** the largest quilt show in the state. Each year over 4,000 people attend this nationally advertised event featuring hundreds of new and antique quilts made by local Amish and Mennonite women. The show is held at the Kalona Community Center, and an admission of $2.50 is charged. Call (319) 656–2240 for more information.

For further insight into the history and culture of the area, visit the **Kalona Historical Village** at Highway 22 and Ninth Street. The village contains seven restored nineteenth-century buildings that include a one-room schoolhouse, general store, log house, buggy shop, and an old railroad depot. Also on the grounds are the Mennonite Museum and Archives, a repository for the documents and history of the Mennonite community in the area (about half of Kalona's residents are Mennonites, members of a religious group who, like the Amish, are noted for their simple living and plain dress).

The best time to visit the village is during its annual Fall Festival, a down-home celebration with plenty of delicious food, homemade crafts, and demonstrations of old-time skills like spinning, weaving, cornmeal grinding, and wood sawing. For me the smells alone are worth the trip: Big pots of bubbling apple butter send a heavenly aroma through the crisp air, a smell rivaled only by that of bread baking in the village's outdoor oven.

The Kalona Fall Festival is held each September, and the Historical village is open Monday through Saturday from April 15 to October 15, from 10:00 A.M. to 4:00 P.M. The rest of the year, hours are 11:00 A.M.–3:00 P.M., Monday through Saturday. Admission is $2; call (319) 656–3232 for more information.

South of Kalona on Highway 1 is the town of Washington, site of several vintage homes and buildings. The pre–Civil War Jonathan Clark Conger House is open for tours from June through August, and the Alexander Young log cabin (built in 1840) is located in Sunset Park just off Highway 92.

Washington is also home of one of Iowa's most unusual enterprises, **Heartland Bicycle Tours**. The company offers guided bike tours throughout eastern Iowa, with accommodations each night in a country inn or bed-and-breakfast. A typical tour is a two- to four-day journey along quiet country roads. You can ride as few or as many miles as you like each day, and van assistance is available if your knees give out in the middle of the trip. All breakfasts and dinners are included, and rental bikes are available.

Heartland Bicycle Tours are given from May through October, with special prices for families, groups, and bikers over sixty. Prices range from $175 to $400 for a complete package. For a free brochure, call (319) 653–2277.

Louisa County

In Louisa County, test your mettle on the **Columbus Junction Swinging Bridge**. A 262-foot suspension bridge made of steel cable and wooden boards, it stretches across a deep wooded ravine and provides a suitably scary feeling as you stand in its center and sway back and forth.

The bridge's nickname is the "Lover's Leap Bridge," a reference to a local legend that says that an Indian maiden jumped to her death in the ravine after hearing that her warrior sweetheart had been killed in battle. The bridge itself was first erected in 1896 so that residents could travel between Third and Fourth streets in Columbus Junction without making a detour around the ravine. Since then the bridge has been replaced several times, most recently in 1921 when a professor of engineering at Iowa State University designed a new bridge for the town. To reach the bridge, follow the signs on Highway 92 on the west end of Columbus Junction.

From Columbus Junction, go east on Highway 92 and then south on Highways 61 and 99 until you reach the **Toolesboro Indian Mounds**. This National Historic Landmark has one of the largest Indian mounds in the state, with several smaller ones nearby. The mounds are the work of Hopewell Indians who lived in the area from 200 B.C. to A.D. 500. The people of this culture are best known for their artistic achievements and elaborate death ceremonies, which led them to build large mounds for their dead and surround them with pottery, pipes, stone tools, weapons, ornaments, and beads. The Hopewell people prospered in the area and then seem to have disappeared by the sixth century A.D. for reasons unknown to archeologists. All that remains of their culture has rested underground for the past 1,400 years.

The Hopewell Mounds at Toolesboro have been known to Iowans since the earliest days of white settlement. The site was designated a historic landmark in 1966, and a visitor center was built in 1968. Here you can learn about the history of the mound builders as well as the explorers and pioneers who settled the area.

The visitor center is open from Memorial Day through Labor Day, Friday through Monday from 1:00 to 4:00 P.M. Call (319) 766–2571 for more information.

Also in the area is the Mark Twain National Wildlife Refuge, a haven for migratory waterfowl and other wildlife. During the fall migration, populations of more than 100,000 ducks and 6,000 geese have been sighted here. The refuge headquarters are located north of Toolesboro on County Road X-61. An interpretive trail into the refuge is marked by signs.

Henry County

Mount Pleasant in Henry County is a town that lives up to its name. A prosperous community of 8,500, Mount Pleasant is an Iowa success story with a thriving economy and friendly small-town atmosphere.

But what makes this town well known throughout the state belongs as much to the past as it does to the present: the **Midwest Old Threshers Reunion,** a celebration of old-time agriculture that draws more than 100,000 visitors each Labor Day weekend. The event began in 1950, when a small group of enthusiasts got together at the Henry County Fairgrounds to exhibit steam-engine equipment. (Before the development of the gas-engine tractor in the 1920s, smoke-belching steam engines provided the power that ran America's farms.)

Today the reunion has grown into a five-day event that draws visitors from throughout the country. Many are drawn by the wonderful old behemoth machines on display here: antique tractors and trucks, electric trolleys, steam trains, and all kinds of engines. Other attractions include live entertainment by nationally known performers, a log village, craft demonstrations, and food tents staffed by local church and civic groups that serve platefuls of ham, fried chicken, mashed potatoes, and various fixings. Take a ride on a trolley, attend classes in a one-room school, learn how to make soap, and watch a horse-pull competition—activities all meant to recall a largely vanished way of life.

If you can't make it to the reunion, the Old Threshers 160-acre site is still worth a visit. The permanent Heritage Museums here house scores of steam engines, antique tractors, agricultural equipment, and tools. There are also a farmhouse, barn, and exhibits on farm women and the use of water and electricity.

**Steam-Powered Tractor,
Midwest Old Threshers Reunion**

The Midwest Old Threshers Reunion is held each year during the five days ending on Labor Day. Camping and motel accommodations are available. Admission is $6 for a five-day pass. The Heritage Museums are open daily from Memorial Day through Labor Day, from 9:00 A.M. to 4:30 P.M. Admission is $2.50 for adults; children under ten are admitted free. Call (319) 385–8937 for more information on the reunion or museums.

Also on the Old Thresher grounds is the **Museum of Repertoire Americana,** one of my favorite museums in the state. The facility houses the country's largest collection of tent, folk, and repertoire theater memorabilia—show business that's in the rural, rather than Hollywood, style. Before the days of radio, movies, and television, hundreds of traveling theater companies crisscrossed the nation, bringing live entertainment to even the smallest towns. This museum provides a colorful introduction to that forgotten past.

The museum owes its existence to Neil and Caroline Schaffner, former owners of the Schaffner Players. The two are best known for their stage characters of Toby and Susie, the wise country bumpkin and his sharp-tongued girlfriend. For nearly forty years their company performed throughout the Midwest, and after they retired they dreamed of establishing a museum to save the memories of early popular theater.

Mount Pleasant and the Midwest Old Threshers Association came to their rescue, and in 1973 the new museum opened its doors. Inside is a fascinating collection of costumes, advertising sheets, scrapbooks, scenery, pictures, and newspapers relating not only to the Schaffners' careers, but to all forms of early American theater. (Don't miss the beautiful hand-painted opera house curtains that were used as scenery for plays.) If you're lucky, museum curator Caroline Schaffner will be on hand to regale you with stories of what it was like to be a traveling performer forty years ago.

The Museum of Repertoire Americana can be visited by appointment only, except during the Old Threshers Reunion, when it is open throughout the reunion weekend. Admission is $2.50. Call (319) 385–8937 to arrange a visit.

Before you leave Mount Pleasant, you might want to grab a cup of coffee at what I think is the most creatively named cafe in the state: the **Goo-Cheez Designer Diner,** just off the town square in downtown Mount Pleasant. As one would expect at a place with such an exalted name, the diner serves delicacies such as seafood fettuccine alfredo as well as more standard cafe fare. The atmosphere is bright and pleasant and the food tasty.

Goo-Cheez Designer Diner is at 100 South Main Street (319–385–3636). Hours are 7:00 A.M.–10:00 P.M., Monday through Thursday and 7:00 A.M.–11:00 P.M. on Fridays and Saturdays. Prices are inexpensive for lunch and inexpensive to moderate for dinner.

Jefferson County

As you drive across southern Iowa, don't miss seeing the campus of the state's most unusual institution of higher learning, **Maharishi International University,** on the north edge of Fairfield. Much of it looks like any tranquil midwestern college campus—until you drive past its two huge, golden domes rising out of the Iowa prairie. The contrast symbolizes the interesting mixture at MIU, which combines traditional academic disciplines with the practice of Transcendental Meditation. Twice each day students and faculty gather in the domes to practice a mediation technique that they say reduces stress and increases their creativity and productivity.

When representatives of the Maharishi Mahesh Yogi bought the campus of bankrupt Parsons College in Fairfield in 1974, many locals worried that their peaceful community would become a haven for leather-fringed hippies. Instead, MIU has helped stimulate an economic boom in Fairfield that has made it one of the most dynamic small towns in the state. Many new businesses have been started by meditators associated with MIU, a number of them high-tech companies seeking to compete on a national level. The boom has earned Fairfield the nickname of "Silicorn Valley," and locals are no longer worried that the newcomers are going to spoil their town.

One of the businesses that has brought fame to Fairfield is the **Great Midwestern Ice Cream Company,** a manufacturer of premium ice cream that easily rivals Häagen-Dazs for richness and taste. Fred Gratzon, its founder, came to Fairfield to be close to MIU and started a small ice-cream business in 1979 to support himself while he decided what he wanted to do with his life. With $10,000 in cash from his mother and several friends, he purchased some used ice cream–making equipment and started educating himself on the mysteries of ice-cream recipes and business strategies.

Gratzon was a fast learner: Today his Great Midwestern Ice Cream is sold in supermarkets, restaurants, and food-service outlets across the country, in the process winning "Best in America" awards from publications ranging from *People* to *Playboy*. All the ice cream is manufactured in Fairfield, using milk from Iowa cows (nonmeditating ones, but peaceful nevertheless).

To sample some of their output, visit the Great Midwestern's small outlet store a block off the town square in Fairfield. In addition to ice cream, there are sandwiches and homemade desserts and cookies for sale here, and during the summer months you can enjoy your meal at a table outside. Prices are inexpensive, though you should expect to pay over a dollar for an ice-cream cone (the price is worth it, especially if you're not worried about your cholesterol level).

The Great Midwestern Ice Cream Company is located at 203 West Broadway Street (319–472–4328). Hours are Monday through Thursday, 9:00 A.M.–9:00 P.M.; Friday, 9:00 A.M.–10:00 P.M.; Saturday, 10:00 A.M.–9:00 P.M.; and Sunday, 10:00 A.M.–8:00 P.M.

Wapello County

In tiny Eldon in southern Wapello County is the **American Gothic House,** a home whose image is one of the most reprinted in the country, thanks to Grant Wood's having used it as a backdrop for his painting *American Gothic.* The picture of the grim pitchfork-bearing farmer and his equally sour wife is one of the most familiar (and parodied) images in American art, and it has brought fame to the modest house that inspired it.

The home's brush with fame was entirely coincidental. While on a motor trip through southeastern Iowa in 1930,

Wood saw the house and made a rough sketch on the back of an envelope of its Gothic-arched window and two long-faced people in front. Later he looked around his home of Cedar Rapids for a farmer who would fit his ideal, but none were quite right. Finally he persuaded his sister, Nan, and his dentist, Dr. B. H. McBeeby, to be his models.

Eldon takes great pride in its most famous landmark, though the home is privately owned and can be viewed from the outside only. Follow the signs through town to find it, and don't forget to pack your camera. (It helps if you have a friend along who can take your picture in front of it, and you might bring a lemon so you can achieve the proper facial expression.)

From Eldon travel north on Highway 16 and then go west on Highway 34. Just before you reach the town of Agency, you'll see a sign for **Chief Wapello's Memorial Park,** a little rest area that marks an important spot in Iowa's history. The park was once the site of an Indian agency (hence the town's name) where the 1842 Sac and Fox treaty was signed to complete the Indian cession of Iowa lands to the U.S. government. This set the stage for the homesteading of Iowa in 1843.

The site is also a reminder of the unique friendship that sprung up between Chief Wapello, a principal leader of the Sac and Fox Nation, and General Joseph Street, director of the Indian agency. After being forced from his home along the Mississippi by the government, Wapello led his people to settle near the Indian agency out of his friendship with Street. The general died in 1840, and before Wapello died two years later he asked to be buried beside him. Their graves rest undisturbed in the park to this day.

Continue on Highway 34 and you'll come to Ottumwa, recognized by the *Guiness Book of World Records* as the "Video Game Capital of the World." In 1983 and 1986 the town was the site for the North American Video Game Challenge. And while Riverside is the future birthplace of Captain James T. Kirk, Ottumwa can claim a famous citizen of its own: Radar O'Reilley of "M*A*S*H" fame. The city also boasts a number of fine parks, several annual festivals, and a number of historic sites.

West of Ottumwa near Blakesburg is the **Air Power Museum,** home to nearly fifty old-fashioned aircraft and the site of an annual reunion of antique-airplane enthusiasts each July. The museum is a labor of love for its founder and president, Bob Taylor, an aviation buff who soloed just before Pearl Harbor, served in World War II and Korea as a crew chief, and then returned to his hometown of Ottumwa to open a flying service in 1953. That same year he founded the Antique Airplane Association, an organization that claims members from throughout the United States and twenty-two foreign countries.

Antique Biplanes, Air Power Museum

At the museum you can see airplanes from the 1920s through the 1940s, plus various flight memorabilia. Most of the planes are civilian craft, with a few home-built ones on display as well. There's also a library for people doing research and renovation on antique aircraft.

The Air Power Museum is open from 9:00 A.M. to 5:00 P.M. on weekdays, from 10:00 A.M. to 5:00 P.M. on Saturday, and from 1:00 to 5:00 P.M. on Sunday. Call (515) 938–2773 for more information. Admission is by donation.

Mahaska County

Oskaloosa, the county seat of Mahaska County, has always struck me as one of the prettiest-named towns in Iowa. It's named after the wife of Chief Osceola of the Seminole tribe, and its meaning is as lovely as it sounds: "Last of the Beautiful." Legend has it that Oskaloosa's husband believed that her beauty could never be surpassed.

A major attraction in Oskaloosa is the **Nelson Pioneer Farm Museum,** a complex of restored buildings developed around the original pioneer homestead of Daniel Nelson, who acquired the land from the U.S. Government in 1844. The land was farmed by the Nelson family until 1958, when it was given to the Mahaska County Historical Society. The Nelson home and barn are both designated as national historic sites, and there are also a number of other buildings open for tours, including a log cabin, summer kitchen, meat house, post office, voting house, school, and Friends meetinghouse. Guided tours are available.

This is also the site of the only mule cemetery in Iowa, the final resting place of Becky and Jennie, two white mules owned by Daniel Nelson that served in the U.S. Artillery during the Civil War. They lived out the rest of their days on the farm and now have a special plot near the museum.

A good time to visit the Nelson museum is during its annual Pioneer Farm Festival held on the third Saturday in September. Over thirty pioneer skills are demonstrated each year, along with special exhibits and musical entertainment. The Nelson Pioneer Farm Museum is located on Glendale Road, 2 miles off Highway 63 (515–672–2989). It is open

May 12 to October 12, Tuesday through Saturday, 10:00 A.M.–4:30 P.M. and Sundays, 1:00–4:30 P.M. Admission is $2 for adults and $1 for children.

Monroe County

The town of **Albia** in Monroe County at one time had the dubious distinction of being known as the ugliest town in Iowa. What once had been the center of a prosperous coal-mining region had gradually slipped into decay and neglect, and years of grime and coal dust coated the downtown's once-elegant Victorian buildings.

Then came Operation Facelift in the early 1970s, when the community banded together to save its historic buildings, using funds that came almost entirely from local sources. Visit Albia today and you'll see a town square far different from the shabby district of years past. Brightly painted, refurbished storefronts, tree-lined sidewalks, and a general air of prosperity announce that Albia is a town that intends to survive and grow. In 1985 the town received a sweet reward for all its restoration efforts when the entire ninety-two–building business district was named to the National Register of Historic Places—the largest such district in the state.

There are a number of particularly impressive restorations in town that should be on your architectural tour of the city. The Perry House at 212 Benton Avenue West is an outstanding example of Victorian Gothic style; Kendall Place at 209 Benton Avenue East was the home of Nate Kendall, governor of Iowa from 1921 to 1925; and the Elbert-Bates House at 106 Second Avenue West is one of four sister homes built in the beautiful Italianate style. Another outstanding renovation is the Barbary Coast Opera House, now used for movies, concerts, recitals, and community theater. And at the Monroe County Historical Museum, housed in a restored trolley barn, you can browse through displays that tell the story of Albia's coal-mining and farming past.

Each year on the weekend before Labor Day, Albia celebrates its rebirth during Restoration Days. A parade, talent show, antiques auction, art show, ethnic food booths, and art show are all part of the festivities, along with guided tours of many of the restored buildings. For more information about Albia or Restoration Days, contact its chamber of commerce at (515) 932–5108.

Appanoose County

During the 1880s Appanoose County was the site of a number of booming coal mines, and some of the lore still remains from those days. Towns like Centerville and Mystic were home to miners with a rich set of superstitions: One belief said that if a miner met a woman on the way to work, he would be killed or injured in the near future. Another common superstition had it that if a miner returned home from work for something he had forgotten, he should sit down and make a wish. Rabbits' feet, buckeyes, and horse-shoes were carried by many miners—and indeed luck was needed to survive the often dangerous work.

After the turn of the century, the coal mines gave out and the area's brief prosperity faded. Today the major draw to the area is Rathbun Lake, the state's largest lake, which was created in the 1970s as part of a flood-control project on the Chariton River. Seven parks line its banks, and there are swimming areas, boat ramps, campgrounds, and picnic areas available for public use.

The **Rathbun Fish Hatchery** was the first hatchery in the country to raise fish under intensive culture techniques. That means that the fish are raised in concrete tanks in which fresh water is continually circulated. The method is undoubtedly successful: The hatchery produces some 160,000 pounds of fish each year. Catfish, walleye, large-mouth bass, and northern pike are all raised here and then released into Iowa's lakes and rivers.

The visitor center at the hatchery is located 7 miles north-west of Centerville and has displays and a film on hatchery operations. You're also welcome to take a self-guided tour through the facility.

Van Buren County

It has been said that the best part of Van Buren County is that nothing much happens here. The county seat of

Keosauqua has a grand total of one thousand people (when everyone is home), and the pace in the county's other towns is just as slow. Visitors agree that the quiet is part of the area's allure—that and an old-fashioned atmosphere that's authentic, not manufactured.

Back in the mid-nineteenth century, however, life was more hectic in Van Buren County. The meandering Des Moines River that flows through the center of the county was a busy passageway for steamboats, and the villages on its banks were bustling ports. Mills, stores, and hotels filled the towns, and an active social life kept both locals and visitors entertained. Unfortunately, the years of prosperity ended abruptly when the U.S. Congress decided that the locks and dams along the river would no longer be maintained, thus making the river unnavigable by the larger boats. Soon the towns settled into faded obscurity, as all but a few residents packed up their bags and moved away.

Within the past twenty years, the area has experienced a renaissance that has preserved its historical character and charm and made it a favorite destination for growing numbers of visitors. Keosauqua is a good place to begin your tour. The name comes from an Indian word meaning "great bend," a reference to the loop the Des Moines River takes around the town. Keosauqua was once a stop on the Underground Railroad and was also a fording spot for the Mormons on their westward trek in the late 1840s.

Today the best-known landmark in Keosauqua is the **Hotel Manning,** a two-story brick structure with wide verandas for watching the Des Moines River flow by. The hotel was built in 1854 and through the ensuing years has withstood no less than four floods. (During the flood of 1947, the owner and her guests were forced to live on the second floor and had to use a rowboat to traverse the downstairs lobby.)

I enjoy staying at the Hotel Manning because it's like slipping into an old, comfortable shoe. The floors creak, the doors don't always match, and there's a delightful air of faded gentility about the place that makes it easy to imagine how it must have been when river travelers stayed here a hundred years ago. The hotel's eighteen rooms are furnished with antique furniture and brightly patterned quilts, braided rugs line the floor, and steam radiators keep the building toasty warm in winter. Downstairs is a cozy bar, and off the main lobby is the hotel's dining room where breakfast, lunch, and dinner are served. Rates at the Hotel Manning range from $25 to $55 a night; call (319) 293–3232 for reservations.

Also in the area is Lacey-Keosauqua State Park, one of the state's largest parks, with more than 1,600 acres. The great horseshoe bend the river makes here offers beautiful vistas for hikers and campers.

Next travel east to **Bentonsport,** a tiny village with a number of restored buildings and stores on its main street. Take special note of the Greef General Store, a structure built in the Federal style in 1853 that now serves as a showcase for local antiques and crafts. East of the store is the Bank of Bentonsport building, where you can find the work of local potter Betty Sedore. She has established a regional reputation with her distinctive "Queen Anne's Lace" pottery. Using hand-dug local clay, Sedore molds the pottery and then presses the wild flower Queen Anne's lace into the clay while it's still wet. The result is a beautiful tracery of lines and flowers. Another landmark in town is the Mason House Inn, which like the Hotel Manning was built in the 1800s to accommodate steamboat passengers. Furnished with antiques, the house contains eight guest rooms. Call (319) 592–3133 for reservations.

Down the river from Bentonsport is the village of Bonaparte, also the site of historic-preservation efforts. In 1989 its downtown area was named a National Historic District, a tribute to the hard work of the village's citizens. A number of attractions here are worth a visit. The Aunty Green Museum was once a hotel (and, according to rumor, a house of ill repute); today it houses a museum and library. There's also a shop featuring the wood carving of local artist Bill Easter.

The best-known restoration here is **Bonaparte's Retreat,** a fine restaurant housed in a nineteenth-century gristmill. Owned by Ben and Rose Hendricks, the restaurant is known for both the quality of its food and its decor, a pleasing mixture of steamboat and gristmill relics, antique quilts, and Navajo rugs. Ben greets all customers at the door dressed in his tuxedo and will willingly bend your ear with stories of the area's past. The restaurant's menu includes steak, pork, and seafood.

Bonaparte's Retreat is open Monday through Saturday beginning at 5:00 P.M. Phone (319) 592–3339. Prices are moderate to expensive.

The last of the Van Buren villages is Farmington, best known for the natural beauty that surrounds it. Shimek State Forest, the largest continuous forest in the state, encircles the village and provides fine hiking, bird-watching, and hunting opportunities.

Lee County

The city of Keokuk is located in the southeastern tip of the state of Iowa and was once known as the "Gate City" because of its position at the foot of the Des Moines River rapids on the Mississippi. In the early days of settlement, steamboats were unable to go beyond this point, and all passengers had to disembark here to either continue their journey on land or board another boat upriver. The city played an important role in the Civil War, when seven hospitals were established here to care for the wounded transported up the Mississippi from southern battlefields. Keokuk's national cemetery was one of the original twelve designated by the U.S. Congress and is the resting place for both Confederate and Union soldiers.

The city's most famous citizen was Mark Twain, who worked here as a young man in the printing shop of his brother, Orion Clemens. Most of the type for the city's first directory was set by Twain, who listed himself in its pages as an "antiquarian." When asked the reason for this, he replied that he always thought that every town should have at least one antiquarian, and since none had appeared for the post, he decided to volunteer.

The *George M. Verity* **Riverboat Museum** will take you back to those days when Keokuk was a busy river port. Built in 1927, the *Verity* was the first of four steamboats built to revive river transportation on the Mississippi. In 1960 it was retired and given to the city of Keokuk for use as a river museum. Today it contains many old-time photographs of riverboats and the river era, as well as other artifacts and historical items.

The *Verity* is berthed in Victory Park at the foot of Main Street on the Mississippi River (319–524–4765). It is open from April through November, from 9:00 A.M. to 5:00 P.M. daily. Admission is $1.50 for adults and $1.00 for children.

Also of interest in Keokuk are the Miller House Museum, once home to U.S. Supreme Court Justice Samuel Miller, and the Keokuk Hydroelectric Power Plant/U.S. Lock #19. When the power plant was completed in 1913, it was the largest electric generating plant in the world. Later a 1,200-foot lock, the largest on the Upper Mississippi, was constructed to accommodate modern river traffic. Visitors are welcome to visit the lock anytime and can tour the power plant daily from Memorial Day through Labor Day, from 10:30 A.M. to 3:30 P.M.

Thanks to the lock and dam, Keokuk is one of the most important winter feeding areas for the American bald eagle. As the birds' primary feeding spots in Canada and Alaska begin to freeze, the birds fly south to find food. As many as 1,400 bald eagles winter along the Mississippi between Minneapolis and St. Louis. Keokuk enjoys one of the highest populations because the lock and dam keep the water below from freezing, thus enabling the birds to hunt for fish.

Eagles can be seen in the area from October to early April, but the best time for viewing them is from mid-December to mid-February. Early morning is the best time, when they can be seen soaring and diving for fish. During **Keokuk Bald Eagle Appreciation Days** each January, the city sponsors shuttle-bus service to and from observation areas, plus seminars, lectures, exhibits, and films on the magnificent birds. The city also puts out a brochure listing prime viewing areas. Call (319) 524–5599 or (319) 524–5055; or write to the Keokuk Area Convention and Tourism Bureau, 401 Main Street, Keokuk, 52632. If you do go eagle viewing on your own, bring a pair of binoculars and stay either in or next to your car. It's important that resting eagles not be disturbed; when they fly off, they burn up energy badly needed during the cold weather.

At any time of year, a visit to **Liz Clark's** is a treat you're likely to remember. Liz Clark's is a gourmet restaurant and cooking school run by (you guessed it) Liz Clark. Born and raised on a farm in the area, Liz has studied cooking in Italy and France and has been named by various publications as one of the Midwest's best chefs. Her cooking school offers courses for students from beginners to advanced, on topics as varied as Parisian bistro classics to traditional barbecue.

You can sample Liz's expertise at a seven-course meal in her restaurant, which is open by reservation only to one party or group each evening. The prices are considerably higher than you'd pay at a local steak joint, but it's definitely worth it for anyone who appreciates fine food. A typical menu may include such delicacies as French country pâté, shrimp in wine and butter, rice and pine nuts, stuffed tomato, mushroom salad with lemon cream dressing, and raspberry crepes with almond cream sauce. Prices run around $25 per person, far less than you'd pay for a comparable meal in New York or Chicago.

Another treat at Liz Clark's is the setting. In 1971 she purchased one of Keokuk's oldest homes, an Italianate house built by a lumber magnate in the mid-1800s. She has completely renovated the elegant structure at 116 Concert Street, and both her cooking school and restaurant are housed here. For more information, call (319) 524–4716.

From Keokuk travel north on Highway 61 to Fort Madison, a river town first established in 1808 as a government trading post and one of three major forts guarding the Northwest frontier. Rozanna Stark, the first white child to be born in the state, was born here in 1810. In 1813 the fort was attacked by Indians and its settlers were forced to flee, burning the fort as they left so that all that remained was a blackened chimney (the chimney is now a monument on Avenue H and Highway 61). The North Lee County Historical Center in the old Santa Fe railroad station in Riverview Park gives more information on the history of the fort and the settlement that later replaced it.

Since the mid-1980s Fort Madison residents have been working to create a replica of **Old Fort Madison** on the riverbank near the historical museum. Much of the labor has been done by inmates from the Iowa State Penitentiary in Fort Madison, who whenever possible have used primitive tools and techniques. The initial work was completed at the prison, and then the log structures were re-erected in Riverview Park, at the site several blocks from where the original fort once stood. Today replicas of most of the major fort buildings have been completed.

A good time to visit the fort is during the Trading Post Days Rendezvous held each Memorial Day weekend. On hand are buckskinners and traders who recreate the days of the old fort. For more information, call (319) 372–5471.

Des Moines County

The Indians called the great bluffs bordering the Mississippi in Des Moines County *Shoquoquon,* a name meaning "flint hills." Many tribes gathered flint from area hillsides in the early 1800s for use in their firearms. Their days in the area were numbered, however, for in 1805 Zebulon Pike landed in what is now the city of Burlington, and within thirty years the territory was thrown open to white settlers. Burlington was the first capital of the Iowa territory from 1838 to 1840 and an important steamboat, lumber, and railroad center in the nineteenth century.

Building a town on the steep hillsides surrounding the river valley required some ingenuity. In 1894 **Snake Alley** was constructed as an experimental street connecting the downtown business district and the neighborhood shopping area on North Sixth Street. This 275-foot-long, zigzagging street rises nearly 60 feet up the bluff and is constructed of tilted bricks designed to allow better footing for horses. The switchback design proved to be less successful than was hoped, however, as drivers often lost control of their horses on its steep curves, and plans to construct more streets on its model were abandoned.

Snake Alley nevertheless proved to be a useful landmark for the city. Horses were "test driven" up the winding curves at a gallop, and if they were still breathing when they reached the top, they were deemed fit enough to haul the city fire wagons. When cars were first offered for sale they had to endure the same test, as auto dealers used Snake Alley to show off the vehicles' power, with prospective buyers clinging in terror to their seats. (Today, students in local driver's education courses are also put through Snake Alley's curves.)

Ripley's *Believe It or Not* has dubbed Snake Alley the "Crookedest Street in the World," and each year it continues to draw many visitors. Today the alley and Victorian homes that surround it have been named to the National Register of Historic Places. You can approach the top of Snake Alley along North Sixth Street between Washington and Columbia streets.

Burlington's three historical museums will give you more background on the city's past. At the top of Snake Alley is the 1851 Phelps House, once home to one of the city's most prominent families. On the bluff in Crapo Park where Zebulon Pike first raised the American flag is the Hawkeye Log Cabin, now filled with tools and household items from the pioneer era. The third museum, the Apple Trees Museum, is built on the site of the first apple orchards planted west of the Mississippi and houses the growing collections of the Des Moines County Historical Society. For information on hours, call (319) 753–2449.

Two annual events in Burlington might also be of interest. One is **Burlington Steamboat Days,** held each year during the third week in June. Music is a major part of the festival, with national rock, country, pop, rhythm and blues, jazz, big band, and oldies groups performing daily on an outdoor stage. Other events include fireworks, parades, sports competitions, and plenty of food and drink. Call (319) 754–4334 for more information.

Another event based in the city is **MADRAC,** the Mississippi Annual Down River Adventure by Canoe. MADRAC's parent organization, Mississippi River Adventures, is based in Burlington and coordinates what has become the country's largest organized canoe trip. The event is held each summer and covers 160–180 miles, with various events scheduled at each overnight stop. (One year the route stretched from Winona, Minnesota, to Bellevue, Iowa; another year it began in Muscatine and ended at Hannibal, Missouri.) Participants are charged $55 per person to spend one to three days with the flotilla, and $75 to travel four to seven days with the group. The fee covers campsites, showers, and transportation of gear from site to site.

Participants agree that MADRAC offers an unparalleled way to experience the most famous river in the country and that some sore muscles and sunburnt skin are well worth the

experience. For information about MADRAC, write to Mississippi River Adventures, Inc., 922 North Third Street, Burlington, 52601, or call (319) 752–4142.

Off the Beaten Path in South Central Iowa

Guthrie	10 Dallas	Polk 9 5 6 8 7	Jasper 2 3 4	Poweshiek 1
Adair	Madison 12 14 13 11	Warren 15 17 16	Marion 20 22 21 18 19	
Adams 26	Union	Clarke	Lucas	
Taylor	25 Ringgold	Decatur 23 24	Wayne	

1. Brenton National Bank
2. Maytag Dairy Farms
3. La Corsette
4. Trainland, U.S.A.
5. Iowa State Capitol
6. Iowa State Historical Building
7. Taste of Thailand
8. Valley Junction
9. Living History Farms
10. Bike Ride to Rippey
11. National Skillet Throw
12. Covered Bridge Capital of Iowa
13. John Wayne Birthplace
14. Madison County Historical Complex

15. National Balloon Classic
16. National Balloon Museum
17. Des Moines Metro Opera
18. Sprint Car Racing Capital of the World
19. Kin Folks Eatin' Place
20. Tulip Time
21. Pella Historical Village
22. Strawtown Inn
23. Great Cardboard Boat Regatta
24. Liberty Hall Historic Center
25. Ringgold County Pioneer Center
26. Icarian Schoolhouse

South Central Iowa

Poweshiek County

When Josiah Bushnell Grinnell, a New York City Congregational minister, asked Horace Greeley for advice in 1853, Greeley responded with a command that has become legendary: "Go west, young man, go west!" For Grinnell, west meant a spot of prairie between the Iowa and Skunk rivers. There he established the settlement of Grinnell, a town founded on two principles: Land was to be set aside for a college campus, and no liquor was ever to be served within its boundaries.

Though the second provision has long since faded into oblivion, the first led to the establishment of one of the most respected liberal arts colleges in the country, Grinnell College. Among its distinguished alumni are actors Gary Cooper and Peter Coyote, astronaut George Simon, poet Amy Clampitt, Harry Hopkins (WPA administrator under Franklin D. Roosevelt), and authors James Norman Hall and Ruth Suckow. Grinnell College is an integral part of town life and sponsors many artistic and cultural events that are open to the general public. You might also enjoy a stroll across its tree-lined campus. While you're there, stop by its library, rated as one of the most comfortable, "user-friendly" college libraries in the country.

Also worth a visit in downtown Grinnell is the **Brenton National Bank,** a 1914 structure designed by the famed architect Louis Henri Sullivan, the leader of what is known as the Chicago school of architecture. His work is considered to be among the most influential in modern design, and the Brenton Bank is one of his masterpieces. (Ironically, Sullivan accepted the commission because his work had fallen out of favor in the major cities of the day.) Known as the "Jewel Box," the bank is a nearly cubical building of monolithic solidity. Above its entrance is a great circular stained-glass window, surrounded by an elaborate geometric frieze. Other embellishments include heraldic griffins guarding the door, additional stained-glass windows inside, and decorative exterior and interior friezes. Architecture buffs from around the country make pilgrimages to Grinnell to see the building, which was one of Sullivan's last commissions before he died.

The Brenton National Bank is located at Fourth Avenue and Broad Street in Grinnell and is open during regular banking hours.

Jasper County

The county seat of Jasper County is Newton, best known as the home of the Maytag Company, one of the world's largest appliance manufacturers. At the Jasper County Historical Museum you can view displays on local history, including an exhibit tracing the development of Maytag washing machines from 1907 to the present. The machine's renowned reliability is supported by the fact that the museum frequently receives letters from people across the nation describing their turn-of-the-century washing machines still in use.

E. H. Maytag, son of the founder of the Maytag Company, established another of Newton's well-known industries, the **Maytag Dairy Farms**. Back in the 1920s Maytag took a liking to Holstein dairy cows and began raising them as a hobby on a farm near Newton. For two decades he won international honors for his prize herd, and the Maytag cows became famous across the country (or at least in circles that kept track of things like prize dairy cows).

In 1940 Maytag died and left his herd to his two sons, who unfortunately didn't share their father's bovine fascination. They decided that the herd would either have to be sold or else turned into a money-making enterprise. Happily, at about that same time Iowa State University developed a new process for making blue cheese. In 1941 the Maytag brothers made an agreement to use ISU's patented process and to have their first cheesemaker trained at the university. Thus the famous Maytag cows began earning their keep for the first time.

The process used today is the same as that developed in the 1940s. Using fresh milk from the dairy herds, the cheese is handmade in small batches and then sprinkled with the blue mold that gives it its distinctive appearance. The final step is six months of aging (twice the amount of time an ordinary blue cheese is aged) in specially constructed caves. The result is a creamy, mellow cheese that has been acclaimed by connoisseurs as one of the country's finest gourmet cheeses.

When you visit the Maytag Dairy Farms you can view a ten-minute video that describes the complete cheese-making operation, as well as the history of the company. After the video, a tour is given of the main office and mail-order packaging building, and visitors are given samples of the unique blue cheese (plus the farm's other varieties as well). If it suits your taste, stop by the company's cheese store to purchase some for yourself. If you're traveling from a distance and don't want to carry it home yourself, the company will ship it for you.

To reach the Maytag Dairy Farms from Interstate 80 west of Newton, take Exit 164 and follow Highway 14 north about 3 miles, and then follow the signs. From Interstate 80 east of Newton, take Exit 168, go north and follow the beltline road about 4 miles until you see the sign. The farms' hours are Monday through Friday, from 8:00 A.M. to 5:00 P.M. and on Saturday from 9:00 A.M. to 1:00 P.M. For a copy of their catalog, write to the Maytag Dairy Farms, P.O. Box 806, Newton, 50208, or call (515) 792–1133.

Another culinary treat in Newton can be found at **La Corsette,** a gourmet restaurant housed in an opulent Spanish Mission–style mansion built in 1909. Owner Kay Owen is a former farm girl who worked as a teacher and horse breeder before deciding to begin her own business as a restaurateur. "I've always loved to cook and entertain," she says. "Eventually I decided to try making a living at what I enjoy most."

Guests at La Corsette are treated to a lavish dinner that's served with impeccable style in the home's downstairs rooms. Six nights a week Kay prepares a six-course gourmet dinner for as many as forty-eight—or as few as two—scheduled guests, with the entree selected by the first caller to make reservations. The one-entree arrangement and single seating for each meal mean that guests can mingle between courses as they explore the home's art nouveau interior.

A typical meal at La Corsette lasts nearly four hours, with ample time to savor each course. The food is innovative and delicious. A typical menu might begin with an appetizer of mussels Provencal, followed by a chilled fruit soup and a beet salade mimosa topped with chopped egg. Entrees include broccoli-stuffed Cornish game hen with Mornay sauce, French veal in cream, and beef tenderloin tips in tarragon butter. Next is a cheese and fruit course (often featuring Newton's own Maytag blue cheese) and then a truly decadent dessert such as triple chocolate mousse with Grand Marnier sauce or floating island with creme anglaise and caramel sauce. Each course is served by solicitous waiters in tuxedos, who also offer selections from La Corsette's wine cellar.

La Corsette operates as both a restaurant and a bed-and-breakfast establishment, with four bedrooms available for guests. The most unusual is a room in the tower dubbed "The Penthouse," with beveled-glass windows on all four sides and a balcony. Each room comes with breakfast served in gracious La Corsette style.

La Corsette is located at 629 First Avenue East in Newton. Reservations are required for dinner, and prices are expensive, with most entrees costing between $25 and $35 per person. Rates for the bed-and-breakfast rooms range from $55 to $90. Call (515) 792–6833 for reservations.

Also in Jasper County is **Trainland U.S.A.,** a must-see for anyone who loves model railroading. Located a few miles north of the town of Colfax, Trainland is the fulfillment of a dream for its owner, Leland "Red" Atwood. After many years of collecting Lionel trains, Atwood tore down his family home in 1976 and replaced it with a building designed to house both a museum and living quarters. Friends and neighbors devoted hundreds of hours of labor to help him turn the building's ground floor into a huge display depicting the development of railroads in the United States.

The exhibit represents three eras of railroading: frontier, steam, and diesel. All the scenery is hand-painted and includes details such as a miniature Mount Rushmore, White House, Statue of Liberty, and Kentucky coal mine, plus a drive-in movie with animated cartoons projected on a tiny screen. More than twenty electric trains operate simultaneously over nearly a mile of track, with the sound of steam-locomotive whistles and diesel air horns playing in the background. It's all a monument to Atwood's lifelong passion, a love that began at the age of five when he received his first model train as a Christmas gift.

Trainland, U.S.A., is located on Highway 117, 2½ miles north of the Colfax exit on Interstate 80. From Memorial Day through Labor Day, it is open daily from 9:00 A.M. to 7:00 P.M. In September, it is open on weekends only. Admission is $3.00 for adults and $1.50 for children. Phone (515) 674–3813 for more information.

Polk County

Think of Des Moines, and the image that comes to mind is of a good, solid, and (yes, let's admit it up front) boring midwestern city. If that's your image of Des Moines, it's time you took a closer look at Iowa's capital. The city is full of historic sites, unique shops, fine restaurants, and other attractions that will keep you entertained on your visit, and you're likely to leave Des Moines with plans to return.

Within the past decade, downtown Des Moines has undergone a renaissance that has brightened its atmosphere and raised its skyline. A major project was the construction of a 2.5-mile skywalk system that links together twenty blocks of the downtown area. Included on the skywalk route are hotels, restaurants, shopping centers, office buildings, residential complexes, and parking facilities, making it possible for you to travel throughout the downtown without ever going outside—an attractive alternative on one of Iowa's cold winter days. (The skywalk system is also the site of one of the state's most unusual sports competitions, the Skywalk Open, an indoor golf tournament held each February.)

A good place to begin your tour of Des Moines is at the **Iowa State Capitol,** one of the nation's most beautiful capitols. It dominates the city's skyline visually as well as politically, with its 275-foot-high gold-leaf dome flanked by four smaller domes. Inside it's a showcase for nineteenth-century craftsmanship and an impressive monument to the artisans who constructed it in the late 1800s. Its cornerstone (a huge prairie boulder from Buchanan County) was laid in 1871, and the building was finally completed in 1886 at a total cost of more than $2.8 million—a figure that must have made conservative farmers of the day shake their heads in disgust.

Some of the country's most highly regarded artists were commissioned to fill the building's marble, stone, and wood interior. Elaborate hand-painted ceilings, exquisite mosaics and murals, and intricate wood carvings have all been preserved, making this an elegant setting indeed for the workings of state government. Major features of the building include the legislative chambers, supreme court, governor's office, and a lovely law library with spiral staircases leading to the shelves of books. Outside, you're welcome to explore the acres of public gardens that put on a continuous show of color from spring through fall. Another good time to visit the Capitol is when the legislature is in session, when you can see up close the lobbying and politicking that go on in the hallways of the grand old building.

The Iowa State Capitol is located at East Ninth Street and Grand Avenue off Interstate 235. It is open from 8:00 A.M. to

Iowa State Capitol

4:30 P.M., Monday through Friday, and from 8:00 A.M. to 4:00 P.M. on weekends and holidays. Free guided tours are given Monday through Saturday. Call (515) 281–5591 for times and information.

Next to the capitol is another of Iowa's treasures, the **Iowa State Historical Building.** Completed in 1987, this dramatic granite-and-glass structure is a stunning setting for the collections of the State Historical Society of Iowa. Visitors enter a soaring atrium-style lobby that ascends to a height of 65 feet. Oak floors, exposed pipes, and large skylights make for an inviting interior, which includes two floors of exhibits, a gift shop and auditorium, and the State Historical Library. The building's $25.4 million cost was met through private donations and $10 million from the Iowa State Lottery, so that no tax dollars were used in its construction.

Among the permanent exhibits in the museum is "The Delicate Balance," a look at how the animals, land, plants, and people of Iowa have coexisted throughout the state's history. "You Gotta Know the Territory," with displays that tell the story of the settlement of pioneer Iowa, is a permanent exhibit that illustrates the museum's new emphasis on interactive displays. Here you can churn butter, scrape animal hides, and play American Indian games. Temporary exhibits, some on loan from other institutions, fill much of the remaining space in the new museum, making this a fascinating place to spend an afternoon browsing through Iowa's history.

The Iowa State Historical Building is located at 600 East Locust Street. Its hours are Tuesday through Saturday, from 9:00 A.M. to 4:30 P.M., and Sunday from noon to 4:30 P.M. Admission is free. For more information, call (515) 281–5111.

Two other stops should be part of your historical tour of Des Moines. The first is Terrace Hill, the official residence of the Iowa governor and one of the finest examples of Second Empire–style architecture in the country. The home was constructed at a cost of $250,000 in the 1860s and was home to several of the city's most prominent citizens for many years. In 1971 it was donated to the state of Iowa, and since then more than $3 million has been spent on its renovation. Much of the effort has gone into refurbishing the home's main-floor rooms to their original Victorian splendor. The lower floor is open to the public, while the second and third floors house offices and living quarters for the governor and his family. Terrace Hill is open from March through December, and admission is free.

Salisbury House is another Des Moines mansion that will bring you back in time—to Tudor England, not nineteenth-century Iowa. The home is a full-scale reproduction of a centuries-old Tudor dwelling in Salisbury, England, complete with a great hall with beamed and raftered ceiling, rich tapestries, Oriental rugs, stained-glass windows, and ornate wall paneling. It was built by a wealthy cosmetics manufacturer who purchased many of the home's furnishings in England and who also collected art objects as well as a 3,500-volume library that includes such treasures as a page from the Gutenberg Bible and a copy of the Kelmscot Chaucer produced by William Morris. Tours of the home are given Monday through Friday at 2:00 P.M.

For a taste of modern Des Moines, a number of attractions are worth a visit. For a quiet treat on a frosty winter day, stop by the Des Moines Botanical Center, a 75-foot dome filled with lush tropical and semitropical plants as well as a variety of major floral shows. The new Blank Park Zoo displays more than 800 animals from five continents in exhibits that simulate the animals' natural habitats. It's open from April through October 15. Finally, the Des Moines Art Center is nationally recognized both for its art collection and for its futuristic architecture created by the internationally known architects Eliel Saarinen, I. M. Pei, and Richard Meier.

To recover from your sightseeing, stop by the **Taste of Thailand,** a local ethnic restaurant that has achieved fame in publications ranging from the *London Times* to *USA Today.* Its owner is Prasong Nurack, a Thai immigrant who was a lawyer in his home country before coming to the United States. Here he earned a master's degree in political science from Northeastern Illinois University and then moved to Des Moines in 1976 to open its first Thai restaurant. His lifelong passionate interest in politics has remained strong, however, and his restaurant has become a favorite gathering place for politicians, lobbyists, journalists, and political staffers, particularly during the Iowa caucus season that kicks off the presidential elections every four years. According to *The New York Times,* "the Taste of Thailand has become Des Moine's answer to Elaine's in New York."

The restaurant's reputation is based on its wonderful, authentic Thai food, huge selection of imported beers, and its famous "TOT Poll." Nurack began polling his customers in 1986 about their political likes and dislikes, offering them ballots to complete as they dined. Since then his poll has expanded to cover such burning questions as whether his customers believe in reincarnation, which talk-show host they prefer, and whether they can touch their toes (76 percent said they could, 24 percent called it a silly question). In the front of the restaurant there's a polling booth for those who wish to make their choices in private; otherwise, you can fill yours out at your table. Each month results are tabulated and posted by the front door.

Even if you're not interested in politics, a Taste of Thailand is a Des Moines institution you shouldn't miss. The restaurant is located at 215 East Walnut Street, and prices are inexpensive for lunch and inexpensive to moderate for dinner. Phone (515) 243–9521 for reservations and more information.

Two other restaurants in Des Moines that are worth a visit are Big Daddy's Bar-B-Q at 1240 East Fourteenth Street and Boswell's at 1409 Harding Road. Big Daddy's has the atmosphere of a fast-food hamburger joint but serves the best ribs in town. Boswell's has become a favorite spot for full, let-out-your-belt-another-notch breakfasts. "Don't plan on eating anything else for the rest of the day," says one Boswell's fan.

For an afternoon of browsing, shopping, and munching, check out **Valley Junction** in West Des Moines. The area was settled by coal miners and was once a bustling railroad center with a wild reputation, but as the importance of the railroad faded, so did the town's spirit. Then in the late 1960s, the area began to come to life again, as small-business owners (many of them antiques dealers) opened their doors in the area's historic old storefronts. Today Valley Junction has become a popular shopping district filled with over a hundred businesses, which include upscale restaurants, fancy boutiques, antiques stores brimming with mismatched treasures, and specialty stores selling everything from lace to jewelry to kitchen tools. On Saturday mornings from mid-June through September, Valley Junction is also the site of a Farmers Market.

While browsing through Valley Junction, stop by Winnie's Toy Orphanage for a present for the children, rent a costume at the Des Moines Theatrical Shop, shop for home-grown Iowa gifts at a store called From the Heart of Iowa, and buy a custom-made neon light at the Creative Frame & Neon Company. Then relax in the friendly, Irish-pub atmosphere of AK O'Connor's (I can personally recommend the tastiness of their chocolate-chip cheesecake), or else grab a home-made ice-cream concoction at The Soda Jerk. A couple of historic sites are also worth a look: The Valley Junction City Hall and Fire Station was the first building on the street to be listed on the National Register of Historic Places, and the Jordan House is an 1850 mansion that once served as a station on the underground railroad. It is now being restored by the West Des Moines Historical Society, which sponsors tours of the home on Sundays at 2:00 P.M. from May through October.

The Valley Junction district is located on Fifth Street and the surrounding area in downtown West Des Moines. Take Interstate 235 to the Sixty-third Street exit, and then go south and follow the Valley Junction signs.

One other stop is definitely worth a visit before you leave Polk County: **Living History Farms,** in Urbandale just west of Des Moines. This is a 600-acre agricultural museum that tells the story of farming in the Midwest, from a 1700 Ioway Indian village to a solar-powered farm of today and tomorrow. In between, several eras are highlighted, including an 1850 pioneer farm, an 1875 town, and a 1900 farm. The artifacts come to life through the efforts of interpreters dressed in historical clothing who recreate the daily routine of early Iowans. On each farm the buildings, planting methods, and livestock are authentic to the time periods represented, and visitors are often invited to try their hand at old-time skills like wool carding and apple-butter making. Tractor-drawn carts transport visitors between the five period sites on a regular schedule, and walking trails through native woodlands are also open between the sites.

Living History Farms garnered national attention in 1979, when Pope John Paul II visited here to deliver a sermon on the bounty of the land before a crowd of some 400,000 people. Today the site has been commemorated with an interfaith Church of the Land.

Throughout the year special events and festivals are held at Living History Farms, from bobsled parties and hayrides to pioneer craft shows and turn-of-the-century plowing exhibitions. On July 4th there's an old-fashioned Independence Day celebration, and during the fall there are several events centered on the harvest. Another popular attraction at Living History Farms is their 1900 farm supper program. From November through April, interpreters prepare and serve authentic meals based on turn-of-the-century recipes. Reservations are required (and the suppers are often booked well in advance).

To reach Living History Farms, take exit 125 (Hickman Road, Highway 6) off the combined Interstates 35 and 80. Its general season runs from May through October, Monday through Saturday from 9:00 A.M. to 5:00 P.M. and on Sunday from 11:00 A.M. to 6:00 P.M. Admission is $6 for adults, $5 for senior citizens, and $4 for children. Call (515) 278–5286 for more information.

For more information about attractions in the Des Moines area, call the Greater Des Moines Convention and Visitors Bureau at (515) 286–4960.

Dallas County

Throughout the nation, Iowa is gaining a reputation as a biking state, largely because of its well-known RAGBRAI (Register's Annual Great Bicycle Ride Across Iowa). The seven-day bike ride is sponsored by the *Des Moines Register* and draws thousands of participants who sweatily toil up and down Iowa's hills for a week each July. A mixture of endurance test, parade, and party, RAGBRAI has become an Iowa tradition that's well loved both by its participants and by the small towns that host the ride each year.

Riding across Iowa in July is one thing, but would you believe a bike ride in February? That's when the small town of Perry in Dallas County holds BRR, the **Bike Ride to Rippey.** It began more than a decade ago when some of the town's citizens declared they were bored one afternoon and decided to go on a bike ride. Now that may be fine in Arizona in February, but you need a high metabolism and a sense of adventure (and some would say a screw loose as well) before you take off on a cross-country bike ride on an Iowa winter day.

Nevertheless, from that humble beginning has grown an annual event that often draws more than a thousand participants—though in exceptionally frigid weather, considerably fewer bikers brave the cold. The trip begins in Perry, where bikers are serenaded by the "BRR Band" playing from inside a school bus. Then, with a twenty-one gun salute, the bikers are sent off on a 23-mile journey to the town of Rippey and back. They are welcomed home again with pizza, a whirlpool, sauna, and swimming pool (and, one hopes, free medical care for any touches of frostbite they may have incurred along the way).

For more information about BRR, contact the Perry Chamber of Commerce, 1226 Second Street, Perry, 50220, or call (515) 465–4601.

Near the town of Waukee in Dallas County is Hawkeye Antique Acres, home to the Central Hawkeye Gas Engine and Tractor Association. The association holds two annual events here that are open to the general public: The Old Time Power and Machinery Show is held on the third full weekend in July, and a Swap Meet and Antique Market is held each Memorial Day weekend. The flea market is one of the largest events of its kind in the country and draws thousands of visitors each year. Hawkeye Antique Acres also hosts a Blue Grass Music Weekend on the second full weekend in August. For more information, call (515) 826–3491 or (515) 993–4124.

Madison County

The little town of Macksburg in southwestern Madison County is the site of one of the state's more unusual events, the **National Skillet Throw.** The event began in 1976 when the town's citizens were trying to come up with a summer festival theme. "Why don't we throw skillets?" someone suggested, and thus was born what is believed to be the only organized skillet-throwing competition in the country. The event is held each June and centers on a stuffed dummy set up in a local park. Teams of competitors take turns throwing cast-iron skillets at its head. (One year, a visiting team from Japan overwhelmed the local champions to capture the title.)

Even if you're not up for skillet tossing, there are other activities going on during the day, including a flea market, parade, chicken supper, and other sports events. Macksburg has found that you don't need much of an excuse to throw a town party. For more information, call (515) 768–2273 or (515) 768–2471.

Madison County is known for more than skillet tossing, however: It's also the **Covered Bridge Capital of Iowa.** Out of the sixteen covered bridges that once stood in the county, six remain and are now listed on the National Register of Historic Places. They were built between 1855 and 1885 and were designed so that their covers would protect the road surface from weathering by the elements. Picturesque reminders of a quieter time, the bridges are a source of pride for this predominantly rural county.

The bridges are also the centerpiece of the Madison County Covered Bridge Festival, held each year on the second full weekend in October. This is one of the state's best fall festivals, in large part because of its lovely setting in wooded rolling hills that blaze with color. You'll be able to view the bridges on one of the festival's guided bus tours and also learn some of the history and legends of Madison County. Other highlights of the festival include old-time craft demonstrations like chair caning and candle dipping, a country-music jamboree on Saturday night, spelling bee, coin auction, pony and horse races, quilt show, and antique-vehicle parade. Proceeds from the yearly celebration go to help maintain the covered bridges.

The Madison County Covered Bridge Festival is held each October in the town of Winterset and is centered around its beautiful courthouse downtown. For more information, contact the Winterset Area Chamber of Commerce at (515) 462–1185.

A year-round attraction in Winterset is the **John Wayne Birthplace,** a modest frame house where the famous actor was born on May 26, 1907. Back then he was called Marion

Robert Morrison, son of a pharmacist who worked in a local drug store. The Morrison family lived in the home until Marion (or John or the Duke) was three, when they moved to nearby Earlham in northern Madison County.

Restoration of the tiny four-room house began in 1981, funded by the local community and by the actor's fans and family, who have donated many items to the site. Since then it has been visited by thousands of people, including Wayne's wife, six of his seven children, and former President Reagan. Two of the rooms are furnished as they might have been in 1907, and the other two contain a collection of John Wayne memorabilia (including the eye patch he wore in *True Grit*).

The John Wayne Birthplace is located at 224 South Second Street in Winterset and is open daily from 10:00 A.M. to 5:00 P.M. Admission is $2 for adults and $1 for children. Phone (515) 462–1044 for more information.

At the **Madison County Historical Complex** you can learn more about the local history of the area. This impressive eighteen-acre historical site contains a new museum, 1856 restored mansion, log schoolhouse and post office, general store, 1870 train depot, blacksmith shop, stone barn, and what is probably the only outhouse in the state of Iowa to be listed on the National Register of Historic Places (made of stone, the privy was at one time wallpapered and heated for the comfort of its users). Also on the property is the Zion Federated Church, an 1881 structure that was moved to the complex in 1988 through the support of local residents.

In the complex's new museum you can view exhibits on local history, including vintage clothing, quilts, farm equipment, and Indian artifacts. In the basement is another treasure, a huge collection of fossils and minerals that the Smithsonian Institution offered to buy before it was donated to the museum.

The Madison County Historical Complex is all the more impressive for being located in a town of only 4,000 people. You can view its attractions on the south edge of Winterset from May 15 to October 15, Monday through Saturday from 11:00 A.M. to 4:00 P.M., and Sunday from 1:00 to 5:00 P.M. Admission is $3.50. Call (515) 462–3263 for more information.

For a bountiful meal before you leave Winterset, try the Gold Buffet Restaurant on the north edge of town. It's known far and wide for a buffet that includes roast beef, ham, turkey, barbecued ribs, fried chicken, catfish, Italian sausage, fried clams, salmon, and herring, plus a huge selection of salads and hot dishes. Prices are moderate and include all-you-can-eat servings. Phone (515) 462–3131 for more information.

Warren County

The county seat of Warren County is Indianola, home to Simpson College and the site each summer of the **National Balloon Classic.** The event is one of the most visually spectacular festivals you are likely to find any place in the country. Each August some 200 pilots are invited to bring their magnificent balloons to Indianola and compete for cash and prizes. Throughout the festival the skies of Indianola are filled with brilliant colored balloons, attracting thousands of visitors who crane their necks for hours on end to view the serene craft. Each morning and evening there are mass ascensions, and during the day special demonstrations and competitions are held. After dark there's a Nite-Glo Extravaganza, when the bursts of flames that power the balloons light up the colored fabrics above them, creating vivid patterns against the night sky.

Other events at the festival include musical performances, a town picnic, arts and crafts show, parade, classic-car show, and a carnival and amusement center. Drawings for free balloon rides are held nightly. A few tips for balloon spectators: Wear comfortable shoes and bring a lawn chair or blanket to sit on. And you'll be sorry if you don't bring your camera along—the sight of the balloons rising above the area's lush rolling hills is unforgettable (each year a photo contest is held, in fact, to recognize the best shots taken during the balloon classic).

The National Balloon Classic is held in early August, and admission for each day is $2 for adults and $1 for children. Event passes, good for the entire ten-day event, are available for $10 per person. Visitors should be aware that weather conditions must be right before the balloons can fly. You may want to call ahead before you leave for the event.

Phone (515) 961–8415 for more information.

If you can't make it to Indianola for the balloon classic, you can still visit its **National Balloon Museum.** The architecture of the new $1 million structure is a reason to visit in itself. The motif suggests two inverted balloons, which are approached through entrance arches that accentuate the feeling of entering a balloon. The exterior is trimmed with blue and yellow ceramic tiles that recall the color, serenity, and gracefulness of balloons.

Inside you'll be able to view exhibits that chronicle more than 200 years of ballooning history. On display are balloon envelopes, inflators, gondolas, and other equipment used in

National Balloon Classic

both hot-air ballooning and gas ballooning. Other items include memorabilia associated with scientific, competitive, and record-setting flights, including trophies, photos, and an extensive pin collection. The gift shop is fun to browse through as well, with its displays of posters, calendars, mobiles, and mementos relating to ballooning.

The National Balloon Museum is located on Highway 65-69 on the north side of Indianola. It is open Monday through Friday from 9:00 A.M. to noon and from 1:00 to 4:00 P.M., Saturday from 10:00 A.M. to 4:00 P.M., and Sunday from 1:00 to 4:00 P.M. Admission is free. Call (515) 961–3714 for more information.

Balloons aren't the only reason to travel to Indianola during the summer. Another attraction is the **Des Moines Metro Opera,** the third-largest summer opera festival in the country. Each season the Metro Opera presents three grand operas, all performed in English, at the Blank Performing Arts Theatre on the Simpson College campus in Indianola. The singers are drawn from the ranks of the country's top young performers and present both classic and contemporary operas. Since its founding in 1973, the Metro Opera has attracted national and international attention for the quality of its performances. Iowans are fortunate to have such a premier cultural resource in their midst.

The Des Moines Metro Opera presents three operas in repertory during June and July. Single or season tickets are available as well as weekend packages that include your tickets, comfortable lodging, and elegant dining. For more information, call (515) 961–6221.

Marion County

The town of Knoxville in Marion County is proud of its unique status in two different areas. Its first claim to fame is as the birthplace of the Iowa flag. A design by Dixie Cornell Gebhart of Knoxville was approved by the governor in 1917 and was first used by Iowa regiments in World War I. (Dixie's home still stands at 409 West Montgomery Street in Knoxville.)

Knoxville is also proud of a slightly racier distinction—its status as the **Sprint Car Racing Capital of the World.**

These vehicles are the small race cars with large spoilers atop their roofs, with engines that can reach speeds of 110 to 120 miles per hour. Drivers have been racing sprint cars at the Marion County Fairgrounds for over thirty years on a dirt track that is rated as one of the fastest in the nation (its surface is a sticky, black clay taken from the nearby Des Moines River). Weekly Saturday night racing programs are held from April through August each year, with the season culminating in the National Sprint Car Championships, an event that draws fans from nearly every state as well as several foreign countries. No less an authority than *Car & Driver* magazine has named the Knoxville championship race one of the ten most prestigious in the world.

In honor of its racing status, Knoxville is in the process of constructing a $1.5 million, four-story National Sprint Car Hall of Fame next to its track. The building will include a museum, souvenir shop, and theater in addition to the hall of fame and booths for race viewing.

The sprint car races are held at the Marion County Fairgrounds off Highway 14 in Knoxville. Call the Knoxville Chamber of Commerce at (515) 828–7555 for more information. Other attractions in the area include the Marion County Historical Village, a complex of nineteenth-century buildings, machinery, and artifacts; and Lake Red Rock, a 10,000-acre body of water with many recreational opportunities.

Somehow sprint car racing and barbecue seem to go together, so once you leave Knoxville, head to **Kin Folks Eatin' Place** (formerly Billy Bob's) in the tiny town of Attica in southeastern Marion County. This may be one of the last places you'd expect to find authentic southern-style barbecue, but one bite of its smoky ribs and you'll be convinced.

For the uninitiated, true barbecue bears as much resemblance to meat seared on a grill as a lightning bug does to lightning. Barbecued meat must be slowly cooked in a closed smoker for many hours to achieve perfection—it's the cooking process, not the barbecue sauce, that gives it its distinctive flavor. They know the secret at Kin Folks Eatin' Place, a down-home restaurant where none of the tables and chairs match and the back room is a made-over garage.

The restaurant's owners are Wyatt McDonald and Ivan Tennyson, who opened the restaurant in 1988. McDonald learned the art of barbecue in Wyoming and returned to his home state of Iowa to open a restaurant of his own. "I figured that if it could work in Attica, it could work anywhere," he says. His hunch proved correct. Since the restaurant's opening, its reputation has spread so far that on some nights the line of patrons stretches out the front door and down the street. The restaurant is so successful, in fact, that it has opened up a branch in the town of Sigourney, with more franchises to follow. (The plans led to the restaurant's recent name change, as another franchise had already taken the name Billy Bob's.)

The secret to success here is delicious food at low prices. For $5.50 you get your choice of meat plus two side orders and a roll. Choose between barbecued ribs, beef brisket, or smoked ham, chicken, turkey, or catfish, each served with a spicy barbecue sauce on the side. All the fixings are homemade, including potato salad, coleslaw, country beans, and fruit salad. For dessert try the heavenly homemade blackberry or peach cobbler with hand-cranked ice cream. The service is cafeteria-style, so the line moves quickly.

Kin Folks Eatin' Place is located in Attica (follow the signs). it is open from 10:00 A.M. to 9:00 P.M. Sunday through Thursday and from 10:00 A.M. to 10:00 P.M. Friday and Saturday. Call (515) 943–2362 for more information.

From Attica make your way north to Pella, a pristine small town that looks as if it could be the set for a Walt Disney movie. The name *Pella* means "city of refuge," for it was here that a small band of Hollanders came in 1847 to found a new city based on freedom. Today that Dutch heritage is visible throughout Pella, especially in the downtown, with its European-style architecture, large windmill in the city square, lovely flower beds, and Klokkenspel, a musical clock with figures that perform four times daily. The gift shops around the square stock imported Dutch treasures, and at Jaarsma's and Vander Ploeg Bakeries you can buy ethnic specialties that include the ever-popular Dutch letters, puff pastry baked in the shape of an S with an almond paste filling.

The best time to sample Pella's Dutch heritage is during its annual **Tulip Time** festival held on the second weekend in May. Each spring the town comes to life with hundreds of thousands of tulips, and local residents dress in colorful ethnic costumes as they host thousands of visitors from across the state. Highlights of the festival include folk dancing and crafts, parades, ethnic foods, and the crowning of the Tulip Queen. Another good time to visit is during the Christmas season, when *Sinterklaas* comes to help the town celebrate the season with traditions stretching back a hundred years.

The **Pella Historical Village** will give you the chance to learn more about the history that has shaped this town. It contains more than twenty buildings, some over a century old. Here you can see items that the early settlers brought from Holland, an outstanding collection of Delft pottery, folk costumes, Dutch dolls, Hindeloopen folk art painting, and a miniature Dutch village. The buildings include a log cabin, blacksmith shop, gristmill, potter shop, store, and church, as well as the boyhood home of gunslinger Wyatt Earp. Another historic site in town is the Scholte House on the north side of the town square, former home of Dominie H. P. Scholte, the leader of the group of immigrants who founded Pella.

The Pella Historical Village is located 1 block east of the town square on Franklin Street. It is open from April through December, from 9:00 A.M. to 5:00 P.M. Monday through Saturday. Admission is $4 for adults and $1 for children. Call (515) 628–2409 for more information.

Another of Pella's attractions is the **Strawtown Inn,** one of Iowa's loveliest lodging places. The name comes from the sod huts with thatched roofs that sheltered the Dutch immigrants during their first winter in the New World. The original buildings of what is now the Strawtown Inn were built during the mid-1800s in the same corner of Pella where the sod huts first stood. In recognition of their historical significance, the buildings of Strawtown were named to the National Register of Historic Places in 1987.

Inside the Strawtown Inn you'll find a pleasing mixture of Old World atmosphere and modern amenities. I like the rooms in the oldest part of the inn best. In the Bedstee Kamer, Dutch bunk beds are set into the wall. The Hindeloopen Kamer is decorated in the style of the Frisian painters, and the Juliana Kamer is a long, narrow suite named in honor of Princess Juliana of the Netherlands, who visited Pella in 1942. In the newer wing of the inn are additional rooms, plus luxuries like a sun room with hot tub. Each morning, guests are treated to a hearty Dutch breakfast of assorted breads and sweet rolls from one of the bakeries on the square, plus cold meats, cheeses, homemade jam, and treats from the Strawtown kitchen.

During your stay at the inn, be sure to book a meal at the Strawtown Inn Restaurant. The atmosphere is intimate and cozy, with tables set in small rooms, each with its own distinctive character. The menu includes such Dutch specialties as *Hollandse rollade* (spiced beef) and *gevulde karbonade* (stuffed pork chop with apple dressing and a mushroom wine sauce). All dinners are served with traditional Dutch barbecued meatballs and Dutch apple bread. For dessert, try the homemade ice cream (flavors include a luscious, rich Dutch chocolate, naturally). The inn is open for lunch and dinner, and prices are expensive.

Next door to the inn is the Strawtown Country Store, a sweet-smelling treasure trove of candles, potpourri, baskets, and gifts, plus a Christmas room that's open year-round.

The Strawtown Inn complex is located at 1111 Washington Street in Pella. Rooms for two range from $60 to $85. For information on lodging, call (515) 628–2681. For information on the restaurant, call (515) 628–4043.

Decatur County

In 1988 the town of Leon in Decatur County first hosted what has become an annual event of widening fame: the **Great Cardboard Boat Regatta.** The race is unlikely ever to rival the America's Cup, but in southern Iowa it draws several thousand people each year—no small feat for a town with only 2,000 citizens.

The rules of the regatta are simple, with all the cardboard boats divided into two categories: those propelled by canoe paddles, oars, or kayak paddles, and those propelled by all other forms of muscle-powered devices or by sails. Among the trophies awarded are the Pride of the Regatta (most creative design and best use of corrugated cardboard), Vogue Award (most attractive boat), Team Award (best-spirited and best-organized group), and the Titanic Award (most spectacular sinking). All the races are held on a 200-yard course on Little River Lake near Leon, and "instant" boat kits are available to those who lack the inspiration to create their own.

Even if you're not the nautical type, the regatta offers other activities that will keep you entertained—a flea market around the courthouse, bingo, children's games, water fights, musical entertainment, and an ice-cream social. The regatta is held in early August each year, and there is no charge to attend (boat owners pay a small entry fee to compete). For more information, call (515) 446–7307 or (515) 446–4816.

In Lamoni in southwestern Decatur County, visit the **Liberty Hall Historic Center,** an eighteen-room Victorian house that was home to the Joseph Smith III family from 1881 to 1906. Joseph was the oldest son of the founder of Mormonism and the first president of the Reorganized Church of Jesus Christ of Latter Day Saints. His father, Joseph Smith, Jr., was assassinated in 1844, and in the years that followed the church divided into two main groups. One group followed Brigham Young to Utah; the other became known as the Reorganized Church and named Joseph Smith III its leader. In the 1880s they established Lamoni as their headquarters, and Smith's home became the busy center of the new church. Though the church later moved its headquarters to Independence, Missouri, Liberty Hall has been lovingly restored to its original decor and today tells the story of the Smith family and the Reorganized Church. Many of the items inside are the Smiths' original furnishings. Also on the property is a schoolhouse built in 1875, plus a museum shop selling Victorian gifts.

The Liberty Hall Historic Center is located at 1300 West Main Street in Lamoni. Admission is free, and hours are Monday through Friday from 10:00 A.M. to 4:00 P.M. and on Saturday from 10:00 A.M. to noon. Call (515) 784–6133 for more information.

While you're in Lamoni, take the time to browse through its thriving downtown, home to over thirty antiques dealers. The area is also well known for its quilts. The first quilting guild in Iowa was founded in Lamoni over a hundred years ago and is still going strong today. The guild holds a quilt show every other year at the Shaw Center on the local

Graceland College campus. Another annual event is an antiques show sponsored by the Lamoni Antique Association on the last weekend in April.

Ringgold County

The story behind the establishment of the **Ringgold County Pioneer Center** in Ellston is a good example of a town turning lemons into lemonade. It seems that back in 1914, two smooth-talking strangers showed up in Ellston saying that they were looking for a place to build a telephone factory. If the town put up the money for the building, the strangers promised, Ellston would soon become the largest telephone manufacturing city west of the Mississippi. "Acme telephones will be in every home," they assured the local residents.

So money was raised, and the carpenters went to work on a large brick building to house the equipment. At its completion a community barbecue was held, and the town's progressive banker advanced the two promoters $30,000 to purchase the equipment and supplies necessary to begin manufacturing telephones. The two promised to return in a few days with the equipment, and the people of Ellston eagerly awaited their new industry. Days passed. Then weeks, until gradually it dawned on Ellston that the two businessmen had sold them snake oil instead of a new factory. The bank folded, and many of the town's prominent citizens lost their life savings.

In 1971, however, the telephone factory was finally put to good use when it was donated to Ringgold County as a museum. Extensive repairs were done, and the interior was filled with items relating to agriculture and the pioneer heritage of the area. In 1975 the National Old Threshermen's Hall of Fame was unveiled, an exhibit dedicated to the memory of the men who operated threshing outfits in years past. Also on the site is a restored pioneer home that was built in 1864 and a rural school.

The Ringgold County Pioneer Center is located in Ellston, at the intersection of county roads P-64 and J-20 in the northeastern part of the county (take the Grand River exit off of Interstate 35). During June, July, and August it is open Thursday through Sunday from 1:00 to 5:00 P.M. and on Sunday afternoons only during May and September. Admission is free. For more information, call (515) 464–2615.

Adams County

Adams County was once home to the Icarian Community, one of the country's most famous experiments in communal living. Its history is now largely forgotten, but at one time the community had an international reputation and following. The story begins with the French reformer Etienne Cabet, who in 1840 published *Voyage en Icarie,* a description of an ideal society where all property was controlled by an elected government. The idea caught the imagination of many in the working classes, and in 1848 Cabet led a group of immigrants from Europe to America to found a new settlement based on Icarian principles.

After settling for a time in Texas and Illinois, the Icarians finally achieved a prosperous, self-sufficient existence on 3,000 acres near the town of Corning, Iowa. They had their own flour mills and sawmills, plus a laundry, bakery, store, pharmacy, and library. Their vineyards and orchards were famous across the state, and the group published an intellectual journal that had a wide circulation in France as well as in this country. By 1876, however, problems had surfaced, and over the next decade the group began to disband. Part of the community moved to California, and the communal holdings were officially dissolved in 1895.

Today there are several reminders of the utopian heritage of Adams County. One is Lake Icaria, located north of Corning, one of the largest lakes in the state. Another is the **Icarian Schoolhouse** that was moved to Corning in 1958. The building houses items relating to the history of the colony and is restored with period furnishings, including a potbellied stove, a recitation bench, and many of its original desks. The building is located on Sixth Street in Corning and is open by appointment only.

More information on the Icarian community can be found at the Adams County House of History at 1000 Benton Avenue in Corning. The building served as the county jail until 1955 and today houses antique furniture and china, a large collection of military and band uniforms, a barbershop and medical office, and a display of farming tools. An entire room on the second floor is devoted to the history of the Icarian colony. The museum is open on Sundays from June through August from 2:00 to 4:00 P.M. Admission is $1 for adults and 50 cents for children. For information on either the Icarian Schoolhouse or the Adams County House of History, call (515) 322–3069.

Off the Beaten Path in North Central Iowa

Emmet 19	Kossuth	Winnebago	Worth	Mitchell

Palo Alto 17 18 | Hancock 20 | 24 25 26 Cerro Gordo | 21 23 22 | Floyd 27

Pocahontas | Humboldt | Wright 16 | Franklin | Butler

Webster 13 14

Calhoun | Hamilton 15 | Hardin | Grundy

Greene 12 | Boone 10 7 8,9 11 | Story 5 6 | Marshall 3 2 4 | Tama 1

1. Mesquakie Indian Pow Wow
2. Stone's Restaurant
3. Watson's Grocery
4. Edel Blacksmith Shop
5. Story City Carousel
6. Hickory Park Restaurant
7. Boone and Scenic Valley Railroad
8. Kate Shelley High Bridge
9. Kate Shelley Memorial Park and Railroad Museum
10. Mamie Doud Eisenhower Birthplace
11. Iowa Arboretum
12. Mahanay Memorial Carillon
13. Fort Museum
14. Blanden Memorial Art Museum
15. Country Relics
16. 4-H Schoolhouse Museum
17. Grotto of the Redemption
18. Sod House
19. Estherville Winter Sports Festival
20. National Hobo Convention
21. Mason City Walking Tour
22. Charles H. MacNider Museum
23. Northwestern Steakhouse
24. Surf Ballroom
25. Clear Lake Fire Museum
26. North Shore House
27. Floyd County Historical Museum

North Central Iowa

Tama County

Tama County is the site of the only native American settlement in the state of Iowa. The word *settlement* (rather than *reservation*) is important, because the land here was purchased by the Mesquakie Indians, not set aside for them by the federal government. Using money from the sale of furs and ponies, the Mesquakie (also known as the Sac and Fox tribe) first bought 80 acres of land here in 1857. In the following years more land was purchased with tribal funds, and today the Mesquakie own nearly 3,500 acres of timberland and river bottom along the Iowa River in Tama County.

The best time to visit the settlement is during the **Mesquakie Indian Pow Wow** held each August. This four-day celebration honors the traditional ways of the Mesquakie people, with various arts, crafts, and exhibits on display, plus old-time foods and authentic costumed dancing. The Pow Wow has its origin in the Green Corn Dance, a religious and social event that was held each year at harvest time. The fresh corn was cooked for feasting, and the bounty of the land was celebrated with dancing, games, and socializing. Around the turn of the century, more and more white visitors began attending the ceremonies, and in 1913 the festival gained its official name of the Mesquakie Indian Pow Wow.

Today the Mesquakie no longer live in wickiups, and the corn harvest is done by machine, but the traditions of the Pow Wow remain strong. The center of the festival is dancing, with members from the local tribe (and often guests from other parts of the country) performing dances that have been handed down for generations. The Buffalo Head Dance, for example, honors the magnificent beast that has played a central role in Indian culture and life, while the Swan Dance mimics the beautiful, rhythmical movements of a swan in the water. For the Traditional Women's Dance, the Mesquakie women don elaborately decorated dresses. The Pipe Dance is presented to honor distinguished visitors and warriors, and the Harvest of Bean Dance is performed by young girls and boys to thank the Great Spirit for the abundance of food for the coming winter.

The Mesquakie Indian Pow Wow is held each August at the Indian settlement 3 miles west of the town of Tama. Admission is $4 for adults and $3 for children. For more information, call (515) 484–4678. At other times of the year, you can visit the settlement and test your fortunes at the bingo operation run by the tribe. Games are run each Thursday through Monday night, year-round. Call (515) 484–2108 for more information.

You can learn more about the Mesquakie Indians and the history of the area at the Tama County Historical Museum at 200 North Broadway in Toledo. The building was built in 1869 and served as the county jail until 1970. Today it houses pioneer tools and utensils, antique toys, musical instruments, furniture, and clothing, plus a display of Mesquakie Indian artifacts.

And while you're in the area, drive to the neighboring town of Tama to see the Lincoln Highway Bridge on East Fifth Street. The bridge was built in 1915 to promote Tama as an oasis along the new transcontinental route of the Lincoln Highway (at that time, most of the highway was dirt). The bridge has a decorative railing that spells LINCOLN HIGHWAY, and is listed on the National Register of Historic Places.

Marshall County

In Marshalltown, county seat of Marshall County, bring your heartiest appetite to **Stone's Restaurant.** The diner is an Iowa landmark, with a history that goes back to 1887 when Ebson Weed Stone, whose parents came to Iowa in a covered wagon, opened the restaurant in a former saloon that still had bullet holes in the wall. Stone's moved to its present location in 1910, a site near the railroad tracks that made it a tempting stop for travelers and train workers. Crews on the railroad used to telegraph ahead to place their orders so that their meals would be ready when they arrived.

Just as it was back then, Stone's is the place to go for homemade, stick-to-your-ribs meals. On its menu are staples like meatloaf, chicken and noodles, and beef heart with dressing. Save room for dessert, however, for Stone's is rightly famous for its feather-light mile-high lemon chiffon pie. Visitors from across the country periodically show up on the restaurant's doorstep to sample the pie's tartness, lured by a reputation that has spread far and wide. (When a local dentist recently crossed the border into Mexico, for instance, the border patrolman looked at his travel documents and inquired, "You're from Marshalltown? Isn't that where they have the restaurant with the mile-high lemon chiffon pie?")

Stone's Restaurant is located at 507 South Third Avenue (under the viaduct) in Marshalltown. It is open Monday through Saturday from 11:00 A.M. to 9:00 P.M. and on Sunday from 11:00 A.M. to 3:00 P.M. Lunches are inexpensive; dinners are moderate to expensive. For reservations or more information, call (515) 753–3626.

Another attraction in Marshalltown is the Fisher Community Center, home to the Fisher Art Collection of late nineteenth- and early twentieth-century paintings and sculpture. Among the works on display here are paintings by Matisse, Pissarro, Degas, and Cassatt. Also of interest in Marshalltown is the Susie Sower Heritage Homestead, a restored Civil War–era home at 201 East State Street. It's open every Sunday from 2:00 to 4:00 P.M.

From Marshalltown, take Highway 30 west for 13 miles until you reach the small town of State Center. On its main street you'll find **Watson's Grocery,** a general store that looks as if it hasn't changed a bit since 1920. The store was built a hundred years ago and was operated as an old-fashioned grocery by Ralph Watson for many years until his death in 1979. At that time his widow locked its doors, and the building remained closed until she died in 1989 and her heirs put the building up for sale. Local townspeople approached the heirs with the idea of turning the store into a museum, but they refused to sell it to them. Instead they scheduled an auction to sell the store and all its contents.

But the people of State Center didn't give up so easily. A fund-raising drive was held, and more than $15,000 in pledges poured in. On the day of the auction, State Center citizens crowded into the little store and emerged successful at the end of the bidding. (When one of the other bidders said that he wanted to use the store as a movie set, the locals told him that they'd let him make his movie, but that they wanted the store.) After the auction came the hard part: Volunteers cleaned, scraped, painted, and refinished the dusty and dirty interior, decorating it with old-time advertising signs and refurbishing it with antique equipment and fixtures.

Today the grocery's solid oak counters and hardwood floors gleam once again, just as they did many years ago. Stop by the store and you can buy antique items, locally made products, old-fashioned candy, memorabilia, and reproductions of the old Watson's aprons.

Watson's Grocery in State Center is open year-round from 10:00 A.M. to 4:00 P.M. Friday, Saturday, and Sunday (and by appointment). For more information, call (515) 483–2458.

Also in Marshall County is the **Edel Blacksmith Shop,** located in the small town of Haverhill, south of Marshall-town. The shop was operated by German immigrant Matthew Edel between 1882 and 1940. Today the building is virtually the same as when Edel plied his craft and is a vivid reminder of the days before mechanized farming was widespread. Here Edel shoed horses, repaired tools and wagons, and manufactured implements like garden hoes and wedge makers. Edel was also an inventor who took out patents on such inventions as a "perfection wedge cutter" and nut plier.

Adjacent to the blacksmith shop is a two-story house constructed in the early 1880s, plus a summer kitchen where food was prepared during the warm months. Like the shop itself, they have been left largely unaltered and help complete the picture of what the life of a skilled craftsman was like some hundred years ago.

Today the Edel Blacksmith Shop is owned and operated by the State Historical Society of Iowa. It is open from Memorial Day through Labor Day, from noon until 5:00 P.M. Saturday through Tuesday. Admission is free. Each year on the first weekend in August, the city of Haverhill sponsors a Farm Arts and Artisans Festival, celebrating the skills and traditions of nineteenth-century Iowa rural life. For more information, call (515) 281–5111.

Story County

To see the only municipally owned carousel in the state, travel to Story City in northern Story County. There you can ride an authentic 1913 Herschell-Spillman merry-go-round complete with twenty horses, two pigs, two chickens, two dogs, two chariots, and a whirling tub, with the original Wurlitzer band organ providing the accompaniment.

The **Story City Carousel** first came to the town when its Iowa Falls owner agreed to let Story City use it for its Fourth of July celebrations. In 1938 the town purchased the merry-go-round, which was used each summer until 1979 when it had become too dilapidated to use.

Instead of abandoning the carousel, however, the town decided to save it, raising the $140,000 needed to refurbish and repair it. A local antiques store and refinishing business took on the laborious task, and in 1982 the gleaming, revitalized machine was once again offering rides in its new home, a pavilion located in the town's North Park.

You can sample the nostalgic joys of a ride on the Story City carousel for just 50 cents. The merry-go-round is open from Memorial Day through Labor Day and is located in North Park on Broad Street. On Wednesday and Friday it is open from 6:00 to 9:00 P.M., and on Saturday and Sunday, from 1:00 to 9:00 P.M. For more information, call (515) 733–4214.

From Story City travel south on Highway 69 until you reach Ames, home to Iowa State University. ISU is one of the oldest land-grant institutions in the country and is a worldwide pioneer in the establishment of agricultural studies on the college level. Some 26,000 students are enrolled here in a wide variety of undergraduate and graduate programs. The campus itself is lovely and full of green areas, with historical markers scattered throughout so that visitors can take their own self-guided tours (ask for a map at the Memorial Union on the south side of the campus). On your tour, stop by the library to see its large Grant Wood murals, and notice the sculptures by artist Christian Petersen that are located throughout the campus.

Two spots in particular should be part of your tour. One is the Brunnier Gallery and Museum in the Scheman Building of the Iowa State Center, where you can view a fine collection of decorative arts as well as traveling exhibitions. Also worth a visit is the Farmhouse Museum, the oldest building on campus and a fully restored National Historic Landmark that has been furnished to reflect the 1860–1910 period. Located on Knoll Road, the museum is open on Tuesday, Thursday, and Sunday afternoons from mid-March through mid-December. For more information on Iowa State University and its attractions and events, call (515) 294–4777.

Before you leave Ames, take some time to explore the rest of the city. Several shopping areas are likely to tempt your pocketbook. Downtown Ames has over fifty specialty shops, including the Octagon Shop, an art store with a wide selection of works by Iowa artists. It's located at Fifth and Douglas. Other unique shops can be found at Shoppes on Grand, an 1890 home filled with stores and a tearoom. Look for it at Sixth Street and Grand Avenue. Campustown, an area within walking distance of the university, also has a variety of shops and restaurants.

No visit to Ames would be complete without a stop at **Hickory Park Restaurant.** To find it, follow the crowds: On any given night it seems as though half the city were dining here. That means that you may have to wait awhile to be seated, but your patience will be amply rewarded. Hickory Park serves succulent and tender barbecued meats, the kind that fall off the bone with a nudge and melt with a tang in your mouth. Its specialty is huge slabs of pork ribs, but its smoked chicken and beef ribs also have devoted followings. Each dinner comes with your choice of two side orders, which include smoked baked beans, potato, coleslaw, applesauce, and macaroni salad. For dessert try one of Hickory Park's sinfully rich ice cream desserts. A chocolate mint marvel sundae is the perfect ending to a meal of barbecued ribs, regulars agree.

As you might expect in a college town, the atmosphere here is casual and friendly. Small wooden booths fill the restaurant's interconnected dining rooms, each with a tinplate ceiling and vintage photographs and signs on the walls.

Hickory Park Restaurant is located at 121 South Sixteenth Street in Ames. Lunches are inexpensive; dinners are inexpensive to moderate. On Monday through Thursday, Hickory

Park is open from 11:00 A.M. to 9:00 P.M.; on Friday and Saturday, from 11:00 A.M. to 10:00 P.M.; and on Sunday, from 4:00 to 10:00 P.M. Call (515) 232–8940 for more information.

Boone County

For over a hundred years, scenic Boone County has been the railroad center of Iowa. At one time this was a bustling coal-mining region, with the railroads serving as a lifeline to the rest of the world. That heritage lives on today in the **Boone and Scenic Valley Railroad,** an excursion train based in the town of Boone that travels through some of the state's most spectacular scenery. The railroad is operated by the Boone Railroad Historical Society and offers a 14-mile trip through the Des Moines River Valley from Boone to Fraser, passing through densely forested bluffs and valleys.

The many train enthusiasts in Boone are especially excited about the newest addition to their railroad, a 116-ton Chinese steam locomotive. The saga of the locomotive began in 1988, when Boone resident Mel Hanson saw a picture of a Chinese steam engine in a *National Geographic* article. Society members called the Chinese Embassy to inquire about buying such an engine and eventually arranged to purchase for $355,000 the last steam locomotive to be built by the Datong Locomotive Works, the last factory in China to build the big steam-powered engines. Then came the tricky part—figuring out how to get the huge engine from China to Boone. Political turmoil in China, a long journey by ship across the ocean, and a major accident in California when the train was unloaded all delayed the delivery of the locomotive, but it finally arrived in Boone in December of 1989. Emblazoned on its front in Chinese characters was the message, "The end of a great Chinese era, the beginning of an American dream." (A Chinese crew arrived as well to explain the intricacies of the train to local engineers.)

The Boone Railroad began offering rides on the train in the summer of 1990 and expects the new attraction to draw increasing numbers of visitors to ride its popular trains. Rides on the railroad last about two hours and are offered from Memorial Day weekend through the end of October.

Regular departure times are weekdays at 1:30 P.M. and Saturdays, Sundays, and holidays at 11:00 A.M., 1:30 P.M., and 4:00 P.M. The fare is $7 for adults and $3 for children. The train depot is located at Eleventh and Division streets in Boone (go north on Story Street through the business district to Tenth or Eleventh street, then west for 6 blocks). For more information, call (515) 432–4249.

A good time to visit Boone is during its annual Pufferbilly Days. Held on the first weekend after Labor Day, Pufferbilly Days is a celebration of the town's railroading heritage and a community-wide festival featuring train rides, a parade, antique-car show, live entertainment, a carnival, sports events, an arts festival, and model train displays. Pufferbilly Days has become one of the largest festivals in the state, with new attractions added every year. For more information, call the Boone Chamber of Commerce at (515) 432–3342.

Another piece of Boone County railroad history is preserved at the **Kate Shelley High Bridge** northwest of Boone, and the **Kate Shelley Memorial Park and Railroad Museum** in Moingona. The two sites are named in honor of a local girl who became a heroine at the tender age of fifteen. In a terrible storm the night of July 6, 1881, Kate crawled across a railroad bridge longer than the length of two football fields to warn an oncoming passenger train of a trestle washout near her home. Two crewmen had already died when a locomotive had crashed at the site, and Kate is credited with saving the lives of everyone on the oncoming passenger train. Kate's bravery did not go unrewarded: As word of her adventure spread, the young woman became a national heroine. A Chicago newspaper raised funds to pay off the mortgage on her family home, and a well-known temperance leader of the day arranged to send the girl to college.

In 1901 the North Western Railroad completed the world's longest and highest double-track railroad bridge over the Des Moines River, a marvel of nineteenth-century engineering skill (the bridge is now listed on the National Register of Historic Places). The span was christened the Kate Shelley High Bridge in honor of the local heroine, and in 1903 Kate was named the North Western station agent in Moingona. She held the position until shortly before her death in 1912. Later the Boone County Historical Society bought the depot and opened it as a museum, recreating a typical passenger station of the late nineteenth century, complete with a period waiting-room bench, potbellied stove, ticket window, telegraph, and a wide variety of railroad memorabilia. A Rock Island Rocket passenger car parked on the tracks nearby is used as a theater in which a tape-slide presentation of the Kate Shelley story is given.

The Kate Shelley Museum is located in the small town of Moingona 5 miles southwest of Boone and is open Sundays from 1:00 to 5:00 P.M. from June through September. The Kate Shelley High Bridge is located 3 miles northwest of Boone. For information on either the museum or the bridge, call the Boone Chamber of Commerce at (515) 432–3342.

Railroads are not the only attraction in Boone County. The town of Boone is also proud of its status as the birthplace of Mamie Eisenhower, wife of the thirty-fourth president of the United States. You can learn about her life and times at the **Mamie Doud Eisenhower Birthplace,** a modest frame house where she was born in 1896. The home had been privately owned for many years before a town committee was formed in the 1970s to buy and restore it. After five years of work, the birthplace was dedicated in 1980. Though Mamie was originally against the idea of saving the house (out of modesty, it was thought), she later donated a number of items to the site. Today it is one of only a few first ladies' birthplaces that have been preserved.

Though Mamie returned to Boone a number of times as an adult, her stay here as a child was brief. Her father, John Sheldon Doud, came to Boone in the early 1890s and established a meat-packing company with his father. In 1897, one year after Mamie's birth, the family moved to Cedar Rapids and a few years later, to Colorado. Mamie met her future husband in 1915 on a vacation in San Antonio, Texas, and began living the traveling life of an Army officer's wife. Later, after eight years in the White House, Ike and Mamie retired to the farm home they had purchased in Gettysburg, Pennsylvania—the first and only home they had ever owned. After Ike's death in 1969, Mamie continued living on the farm until shortly before her death in 1979.

Visit the birthplace today and you'll gain more insight into the life of the first lady and her husband. The home has

Mamie Doud Eisenhower Birthplace

been restored to the 1890s period and contains many furnishings that were donated by Mamie's family. The master bedroom has its original furniture, including the bed in which Mamie was born, and there is also a library of Eisenhower-related materials.

The Mamie Doud Eisenhower Birthplace is located at 709 Carroll Street in Boone. Hours are from 1:00 to 5:00 P.M. Tuesday through Sunday during April and May and from 12:30 to 5:00 P.M. daily from June through October. Admission is $2 for adults and 50 cents for children. For more information, call (515) 432–1896.

For a peaceful place to recover from all your sightseeing, visit the **Iowa Arboretum,** southeast of Boone near the town of Luther. The arboretum is a new educational facility unlike any other in Iowa. Located on 340 acres in rural Boone county, it contains hundreds of species of trees, shrubs, and flowers in a quiet, scenic setting. Its main goal is to help Iowans appreciate and better understand plant life. Here you can learn which plants are best adapted to the soils and climate of Iowa and how to use these plants properly for landscaping, gardening, conservation, and other purposes. The arboretum also serves as an outdoor laboratory for testing the hardiness and adaptability of newly introduced plants and a center for the preservation of rare and endangered plant species.

A vital part of the arboretum is its forty-acre Library of Living Plants, where you can view varieties of cultivated trees, shrubs, and flowers. Plants with similar uses are grouped together—small shade trees are located in one area, for example, and trees useful for windbreaks in another. With this arrangement, you can quickly "look up" the best plant for your needs.

The arboretum also contains over 300 acres of forest, prairie, and meadow, with trails that pass by scenic over-looks, deep ravines, and streams. Labels identify the native trees, shrubs, and wild flowers, and illustrated brochures will help you plan your own self-guided tour. Along the way you're likely to see some of the deer, birds, and wild turkey that make their home here. Guided tours and educational programs are also offered.

The Iowa Arboretum is open every day of the year from sunrise to sunset, and admission is free. To arrange a guid-ed tour, call (515) 795–3216. The arboretum is located about 30 miles northwest of Des Moines, 2½ miles west of the town of Luther on County Road E-57.

Greene County

In Jefferson, the county seat of Greene County, pay a visit to the **Mahanay Memorial Carillon,** a 162-foot structure topped by fourteen cast bells. Take the elevator to the obser-vation platform and you can see a view of seven counties. The tower was built with funds from the estate of William and Dora Mahanay, both residents of Jefferson. William was a sales representative for a surgical instrument company as well as the owner of a substantial amount of Green County farmland. When he died, he specified that his estate be used for the construction of a tower on the southwest corner of the courthouse square.

The bells on top of the tower were made and installed by a Chicago company. The largest, middle C, weighs 4,700 pounds and is 5 feet in diameter. The smallest is G, which weighs only 198 pounds. Concerts are played several times each day, as Mr. Mahanay wished.

The Mahanay Tower is located on the downtown square in Jefferson (it's difficult to miss) and is open to the public from May 15 to September 15 from 1:30 to 6:30 P.M. daily.

Also in Jefferson is the Telephone Museum, housing a collection of antique telephone equipment. It's located 1 block east of Highway 4 at 105 West Harrison Street and is open Monday through Friday from 9:00 A.M. to 5:00 P.M. On the north side of the town square, you'll find the Greene County Historical Society Museum, with displays of local history and artifacts.

Webster County

The town of Fort Dodge is the county seat of Webster County, though if a certain wrestling match in 1856 had turned out differently, the town wouldn't be able to claim the privilege.

The story begins when John F. Duncombe, described in a newspaper of the day as "an engine in pants," arrived in Fort Dodge in 1855. At that time Fort Dodge was only a tiny settlement in contrast to the nearby thriving town of Homer. Duncombe, however, spearheaded an effort to have Fort Dodge named as the county seat. The citizens of Homer naturally objected, and an election was held to determine which town would get the coveted distinction. When the votes were counted, it was discovered that both sides had stuffed the ballot box—but that the citizens of Fort Dodge were more successful in their voting fraud, as their town came out the winner. John D. Maxwell, the leader of the Homer faction, was furious. Then someone made the suggestion that Maxwell and Duncombe settle the issue with a wrestling match. For an hour the two battled it out in Homer's public square in front of a large crowd. Duncombe was declared the winner, and Fort Dodge was named the county seat and as a result became the leading commercial center in the area. Fort Dodge has good reason to be grateful for the athletic prowess of John F. Duncombe.

Fort Dodge's history has many more colorful episodes,

and the best place to learn about them is at the city's **Fort Museum.** The site is a recreation of Fort Williams, a garrison built in 1862 to protect local residents from Indian raids. The fort is considered to be one of the finest pioneer museums in the Midwest and contains a complete frontier village with stockade, blockhouse, soldiers' quarters, general store, blacksmith shop, one-room school, log chapel, and drug store, all with period furnishings. Also on display are exhibits on military and pioneer history, plus the National Museum of Veterinary Medicine, the first of its kind in the country.

Various special events are held at the Fort Museum, including a Craftsmen's Weekend and Fall Harvest Festival. The highlight of the year comes the first weekend in June, when the fort serves as the focal point for Frontier Days, a citywide celebration of Fort Dodge's past. The event features a parade, rodeo, Buckskinner's Rendezvous, carnival, live music, historic home tours, antiques fairs, and more.

The Fort Museum is located ¼ mile east of the junction of Highways 169 and 20. It is open from May through October from 9:00 A.M. to 6:00 P.M. daily. Admission is $3 for adults, $2 for ages 13–18, and $1 for ages 6–12. For more information, call (515) 573–4231.

Also in Fort Dodge is the **Blanden Memorial Art Museum,** the first permanent art facility in the state of Iowa. You're likely to be surprised by the remarkable diversity and quality of its collection, which includes such treasures as Chagall's *The Fantastic Horsecart* (one of the painter's personal favorites), Miro's *The Cry of the Gazelle at Dawn,* and Maurice Prendergast's *Central Park,* plus bronzes by Henry Moore, a Calder mobile, and a collection of non-Western art highlighted by Asian art from the seventeenth through nineteenth centuries, pre-Columbian art, and tribal objects from North America and Africa. The museum also sponsors traveling exhibits and art classes for both adults and children.

The museum was founded in 1930, a gift to the community from former Fort Dodge mayor Charles Granger Blanden in memory of his wife. Since then other benefactors have donated money and works of art to the museum, including the well-known Philadelphia art collector Albert Barnes.

The Blanden Art Museum is located at 920 Third Avenue South in Fort Dodge. It is open on Tuesday, Wednesday, and Friday from 10:00 A.M. to 5:00 P.M.; on Thursday from 10:00 A.M. to 8:30 P.M.; and on Saturday and Sunday from 1:00 to 5:00 P.M. Admission is free. For more information, call (515) 573–2316.

Hamilton County

In the state of Iowa you'll find many small towns, but none smaller than **Country Relics.** On their farm near Stanhope, Varlen and Fern Carlson have created a miniature village that's just the right size for young children, though adults are invited to duck their heads and visit too. It all started in 1979 when the Carlsons bought a miniature house at an auction, thinking that their grandchildren would enjoy playing in it. Their grandsons, however, said that they'd rather have a barn, so Varlen obligingly had one built to match the house. "Things just sort of took off from there," he explains.

Visit the Carlson farm today and you'll see that the homestead has expanded to include a schoolhouse, general store, and church. In the barn is a cow stanchion and horse stall, complete with a tiny milk can and miniature bales of hay in the loft. The church contains four cut-down pews and stained-glass windows, while the house has a small cast-iron stove and a diminutive table, cupboard, and cooking utensils. The general store is packed with hundreds of miniature supplies.

The Carlsons have furnished their village with items found at area flea markets and auctions, and they devote many hours each week to improving it in addition to working their regular jobs (Varlen is a farmer, and Fern works at Iowa State University). "Eventually Fern hopes to quit work and use this as her retirement plan," says a smiling Varlen, who has seen firsthand what can grow from small beginnings.

Country Relics is located 1½ miles north of Stanhope on Highway 17. It's open from May through September, Friday through Sunday from 1:00 to 6:00 P.M. (as well as by appointment). Admission is $2 for adults and $1 for children. For more information, call (515) 826–3491.

Wright County

In the center of Wright County you'll find the town of Clarion, home to the **4-H Schoolhouse Museum.** The museum, located in the town's Gazebo Park, is housed in the turn-of-the-century schoolhouse where O. H. Benson, superintendent of schools for Wright County, originated the idea for the emblem of the 4-H Clubs in 1907. The four-leaf clover of the youth organization is a familiar sight to most Iowans, and Clarion takes great pride in its status as its birthplace.

Inside the museum you'll see various displays on 4-H memorabilia and history, including 4-H uniform style changes through the years. Other displays take you back in time to the days of the one-room country schoolhouse. The museum is open daily from June through August from 1:00 to 5:00 P.M., with free admission. For more information, call (515) 532–2256.

Palo Alto County

Located in southeastern Palo Alto County, the town of West Bend is known across the country for its **Grotto of the Redemption.** Each year more than 100,000 visitors travel to see the grotto, which is believed to be the largest collection of minerals and semiprecious stones concentrated in any one spot in the world (the shrine's estimated geological value is over $2.5 million).

The grotto was the lifetime work of Father Paul Dobberstein, who started its construction in 1912. As a young seminary student he suffered a serious illness and vowed that if he recovered, he would erect a shrine to the Virgin Mary. For forty-two years he labored to build the grotto in West Bend, setting into concrete ornamental rocks and gems from around the world. Since his death in 1954, his work has been continued by Father Louis Greving.

Today the Grotto of the Redemption covers an area the size of a city block. Contained within its twisting walls and encrusted caverns are nine separate grottos, each portraying some scene from the life of Christ. Highlights include a replica of Michelangelo's *Pieta* and a life-size statue of Carrara marble portraying Joseph of Arimathea and Nicodemus laying Jesus into the tomb. Adjacent to the grotto is St. Peter and Paul's Church, which includes a Christmas Chapel that is considered to be Father Dobberstein's finest work. It contains a Brazilian amethyst that weighs over 300 pounds. The church's main altar (a first-place winner at the Chicago World's Fair in 1893) is of hand-carved birds-eye maple.

The grotto is financed by the free-will donations of visitors, and hourly tours are given from June to October 15 (though the grotto is open for viewing year-round). The Grotto Restaurant serves inexpensive, home-cooked meals from 11:00 A.M. to 2:30 P.M. in season. Camping and motel facilities are also available. The grotto is located two blocks off Highway 15 at the north end of West Bend and is open from 9:00 A.M. to 5:00 P.M. daily. For more information, call (515) 887–2371.

Also of interest in West Bend is the **Sod House,** a home built of earth and managed by the West Bend Historical Society to help preserve part of the pioneer heritage of the area. At one time sod houses could be found throughout the prairie states, for in a land of few trees they were a quick and inexpensive answer to the housing needs of new settlers. A sod home cost between $15 and $30 to construct, and its thick walls and roof were good insulation against the heat of summer and cold of winter. The sod house era in Iowa lasted only thirty years, from the 1850s to the 1880s. It ended when the expansion of the railroad made lumber cheap enough to be used as a common building material.

The Sod House in West Bend will give you the chance to experience what life was like for most of the early pioneer settlers on the plains. It is located on Highway 15, one block east of the business district in West Bend, and is open every Sunday from 1:30 to 4:00 P.M. from Memorial Day through Labor Day. There is no admission charge. The historical society also operates a country schoolhouse and a historical museum, both of which have the same hours as the Sod House. For more information, call (515) 295–2138.

The town of Emmetsburg in the center of Palo Alto County is also worth a visit, particularly if you have a bit of Irish in your background. The town was settled by Irish immigrants and named in honor of Robert Emmet, the Irish patriot who was executed by the English in 1803. The customs and heritage of the old country remain strong in Emmetsburg, especially during its annual St. Patrick's Day celebration. This three-day festival includes a Miss Shamrock Pageant, marathon run, banquet, dances, luncheons, and various entertainment.

At any time of year, you may wish to place an order at the Blarney Canning Factory in Emmetsburg. The company produces two products: cans of pure blarney and cans of blarney repellent. Both can be ordered for $1 per can or $5 for the economy six-pack size. For ordering information, write to the St. Patrick's Association, 1013 Broadway, Emmetsburg, 50536. (For those who prefer their blarney in solid form, visit Emmetsburg's courthouse square to see a piece of the original Blarney Stone.)

Emmet County

The town of Estherville is named after Esther Ridley, mother of the first white child born in Emmet County. The town was once the site of Fort Defiance, a structure built in 1862 to protect local residents against Indian attacks. The expected Indian raids never came, but something else did: In 1879 a huge meteor fell from the sky near Estherville, breaking into three pieces in an explosion that caused cattle to stampede, windows to break, and townspeople to fear for their lives. Today pieces of the famous Estherville meteor can be found in museums from Paris to Boston. You can also see a specimen on display in the Estherville Public Library.

There's more to do in Estherville than wait for the sky to fall, however. Today the town is best known for its **Estherville Winter Sports Festival,** held each year on the first full weekend in February. For more than twenty years the town has been staging this exuberant celebration of the cold, a sure-fire cure for the winter doldrums. One of the most popular events each year is the Snow and Ice Sculpture Contest. Entries can be found scattered throughout the town, though the best viewing place is the area around the library and courthouse. Among the past winners were a 50-

foot-long tyrannosaurus and a 30-foot-long triceratops—animals that unfortunately (like all of these frigid masterpieces) didn't last past the first thaw.

Other events include downhill skiing at the local Riverside Hills Ski Area, snowmobile racing, an art show and flea market, quilt show, inner tube and mountain bike races, and a Snowball Dance. A snowmobile torchlight parade is held in the evening, as are various musical events. Food plays a large role in the festivities: During the five-day celebration you can attend a spaghetti supper, brat-and-beer Fireside Fest, omelet breakfast, chili feed, and pancake supper. At the end of the festival, most people have eaten enough food to last the rest of the winter.

For more information about the Estherville Winter Sports Festival, call the Association of Business and Industry in Estherville at (712) 362–3541.

Hancock County

Located in central Hancock County, the small town of Britt plays host each August to one of the state's most unusual attractions: the **National Hobo Convention.** These aren't imitation hoboes, either, but the genuine article. They've been coming to Britt's hobo convention since 1900. Over the years their numbers have dwindled, and by now most of them are well past middle age, but each year they return to Britt to swap stories, meet old friends, and enjoy the hospitality of the town.

Britt first hosted the convention in 1900, eager to gain some publicity for the town and show the rest of the world that "Britt was a lively little town capable of doing anything larger cities could do." The national media did indeed report on the convention, not realizing that the town was serious in its intentions until hundreds of hoboes began arriving for the event. The travelers were treated to games and sports competitions, musical performances, and a clean place to stay, and newspapers around the country gave Britt the publicity it had hoped for.

Though the 1900 convention was declared a rousing success, it wasn't until 1933 that Britt once again hosted the convention. Some townspeople were reluctant to sponsor the event again, but they were won over by those who pointed out that the convention was for hoboes, not tramps or bums. A hobo is defined as a migratory worker who is willing to work to pay his way; a tramp is a traveler who begs for food rather than works for it; and a bum is too lazy either to work or to roam around. At a time when many people were out of work and homeless, a hobo was seen as an honorable—even romantic—character.

The town agreed to host the convention again and renewed a tradition that continues to this day. Through the years the event has grown to include more activities, from the crowning of a hobo king and queen to the serving of free mulligan stew. Hoboes like Mountain Dew, Hardrock Kid, and Fry Pan Jack have become legendary in Britt, though today fewer and fewer of their brethren come to the event each year. A new breed is taking their place, however: "yuppie hoboes," weekend travelers who love the open road but still have stable jobs. Both groups gather in Britt once a year to renew their ties to each other and the traveling life.

You don't have to be a hobo to attend the convention, however. Visitors are welcomed, and the town offers a full slate of activities for their amusement: a flea market, parade, antique and classic car show, musical entertainment, art show, carnival, and fireworks display. Visitors are welcome to stop by the "hobo jungle" (the area where the hoboes camp) to listen to storytelling and singing and learn more about life on the road.

The National Hobo Convention is held each year on the second weekend in August, and admission is free. For more information, call the Britt Chamber of Commerce at (515) 843–3867.

Cerro Gordo County

Cerro Gordo County draws its name from a battlefield of the Mexican War and was settled by pioneers of the Masonic Order. Its county seat was originally named *Shibboleth*, which was eventually changed to the less forbidding name of Mason City. The town is perhaps best known as the birthplace of Meredith Wilson, who wrote the book, lyrics, and music for the award-winning musical *The Music Man.* According to local legend, the inspiration for the play came from the North Iowa Band Festival, a yearly institution in Mason City since 1928. Held the first weekend in June, the festival draws marching bands from throughout Iowa and the Midwest who fill the town with the sound of music.

Mason City is also known for its Prairie school architecture, designed chiefly by Walter Burley Griffin and Barry Byrne of the Chicago office of the famed architect Frank Lloyd Wright. The city is credited with having one of the finest collections of Prairie school architecture to be found anywhere, a style known for its open, flowing designs, low roofs, and use of natural materials. The Rock Glenn–Rock Crest development is a district of eight such houses built between 1912 and 1917, and other examples can be found throughout the city.

The best way to see these architectural treasures is on a **Mason City Walking Tour.** The Mason City Convention and Visitors Bureau puts out a detailed booklet that will guide you on your walk, with photographs of the significant landmarks and explanations of their architecture. Thirty-seven buildings are described, as well as the Music Man Footbridge over Willow Creek. Copies of the guide are available for $1 at the Convention and Visitors Bureau at 15 First Street NE. For more information, call (515) 423–1490.

On your tour of the city, you should plan a visit to the **Charles H. MacNider Museum.** Housed in a handsome English Tudor–style building, the museum has a permanent collection focusing on American art and boasts works by such well-known artists as Thomas Hart Benton, Grant Wood, Alexander Calder, Moses Soyer, and Adolph Gottlieb. Another highlight of the museum is its collection of Bil Baird puppets and memorabilia. Baird was a native of Mason City and famous puppeteer whose creations appeared in the theater, in films, and on television for more than fifty years. His puppets starred in the Ziegfeld Follies, appeared in the movie *The Sound of Music,* and performed on television for Ed Sullivan, Jack Paar, and Sid Caesar. In 1980 Baird donated a major collection of his work to the MacNider Museum, including some 400 puppets and marionettes.

The Charles H. MacNider Museum is located at 303 Second Street SE in Mason City. Its hours are from 10:00 A.M. to 9:00 P.M. on Tuesday and Thursday; from 10:00 A.M. to 5:00 P.M. on Wednesday, Friday, and Saturday; and on Sunday from 1:00 to 5:00 P.M. Admission is free. For more information, call (515) 421–3666.

Two other museums in Mason City are the Kinney Pioneer Museum and Van Horn's Antique Truck Museum, where you can see one of the nation's largest collections of pre-1930 trucks. For more information, contact the Mason City Convention and Visitors Bureau at (515) 423–1490.

Another Mason City institution is the **Northwestern Steakhouse,** purveyor of tender steaks and various Greek specialties. Its owner, Tony Papouchis, the son of a Greek Orthodox priest, came to the United States in 1912. In 1920 he opened the Evia Cafe, named after his home island in the Greek isles, a business he later sold so that he could open the Northwestern Steakhouse. In the Depression era he sold more chicken and ribs than the more expensive steaks, but in the years since then steaks have become the menu's staple. Greek specialties are also served here on Sunday nights, from *dolmathes* (stuffed grape leaves) to Greek chicken roasted with lemon and Greek herbs.

Though his age is drawing close to one hundred, Tony is still an active force in the business. His sons John and George are gradually taking over the restaurant from him and have opened two additional restaurants in Des Moines and Ames. The secret to their success: "Keep people happy and they'll keep coming back," says John.

Northwestern Steakhouse is located at 304 Sixteenth Street NW in Mason City. Hours are from 5:00 to 10:00 P.M. daily, and prices are moderate. Call (515) 423–5075 for more information.

Just west of Mason City on Highway 18 is Clear Lake, one of the state's most popular recreation areas. The lake itself is one of the few spring-fed lakes in Iowa, a lovely 3,600-acre expanse of water that draws boat and fishing enthusiasts, water-skiers, swimmers, and confirmed beach bums all summer. Even in winter the area is a popular tourist spot, with cross-country skiing, snowmobiling, and ice fishing for those who don't mind the cold.

The water is not the only attraction in Clear Lake. In the downtown area you'll find a number of antiques stores and specialty shops, and during the summer months semiprofessional theater productions are offered. Boat cruises and rides on an electric railway are popular as well. One of the town's more unusual annual events is the Antique and Classic Boat Show held each July. The show is sponsored by the local chapter of the Antique and Classic Boat Society, an organization dedicated to preserving and restoring wooden boats from the 1920s to 1960s. "A true boat is made out of wood and love, and all the rest are toys," says one member who, like his comrades, derisively describes fiberglass boats as "plastic." Attending one of their shows is like visiting a nursery full of proud parents, all of them eager to show off their babies. The boats are displayed on land and make an impressive sight with their wooden exteriors gleaming with many layers of varnish and chrome so polished it can blind you.

The best way to enjoy the boat show is to find the owners of a boat and ask them about their hobby. Before long you'll be shown a scrapbook full of pictures of the restoration process, and if you're lucky maybe you'll get a ride on one of these grand relics from an earlier day. For more information on the Antique and Classic Boat Show, call (515) 279–6442 or the Clear Lake Chamber of Commerce at (515) 357–2159.

History of another sort lives again at the **Surf Ballroom** in Clear Lake. The ballroom is best known as the site of the last performances given by rock 'n' roll legends Buddy Holly, Ritchie Valens, and J. P. "The Big Bopper" Richardson. Following their concert, the three were killed in the nearby crash of their small plane in the early morning hours of February 3, 1959—an event that became the basis for Don McLean's hit song "American Pie." In 1988 a monument was erected in their memory outside the Surf, and their music lives on in an annual memorial concert. For devoted rock 'n' roll fans, the Surf has become a landmark on the same order as The Cavern in Liverpool where the Beatles got their start. People from around the country make pilgrimages here to relive the memories.

Even without the Buddy Holly connection, the Surf is worth a visit on its own. At a time when most ballrooms have gone the way of the horse and buggy, the Surf is a living reminder of the Big Band era, when swing was king. Today it books a variety of music and dance bands, from country to big band to fifties and sixties classics. (The ballroom also serves food on most dance nights.) The Surf Ballroom is located at 460 North Shore Drive in Clear Lake. For more information, call (515) 357–6151.

Clear Lake is also home to the **Clear Lake Fire Museum.** The facility opened in 1986 and depicts a fire station from the early 1900s. Inside you can see some of Clear Lake's earliest firefighting equipment, along with other antique firefighting memorabilia. Highlights of the museum include the town's 1924 Ahrens-Fox fire truck, an 1883 hand-pulled hose cart, fire bell, antique fire extinguishers, photographs, and brass poles.

The Clear Lake Fire Museum is located at 112 North Sixth Street, ½ block north of the fire station. It is open from Memorial Day through Labor Day on Saturdays and Sundays from 1:00 to 5:00 P.M. Admission is free. For more information, call (515) 357–2159.

Clear Lake boasts several fine bed-and-breakfasts where you can stay as you explore the area. One of my favorites is the **North Shore House,** a cottage on the north side of the lake owned by Jay and Ruby Black. The Blacks used to live in Des Moines and traveled north to Clear Lake just for the summer months, but they loved the area so much that they made it their permanent home in 1988. Their home is a 1920s vintage rustic cottage that had fallen into disrepair, and Jay and Ruby spent years fixing it up before it was liveable year-round. Today you'd never suspect its dilapidated past. Light, airy, and comfortable, the house is furnished in a modern style, with antique boat parts decorating the walls. The patio has a lovely view of the lake and is the perfect place to enjoy a delicious breakfast. You'll find the Blacks to be friendly hosts, people who obviously enjoy their part-time business.

The North Shore House is located at 1519 North Shore Drive in Clear Lake and has two rooms open to visitors, each with a private bath. Rates range from $45 to $75 per night and include a full breakfast. For reservations, call (515) 357–4443.

Floyd County

In 1968 Charles City, the county seat of Floyd County, was devastated by a tornado that destroyed nearly one-third of the community's buildings. Instead of giving up, the people of Charles City chose to rebuild their town, so that today it is one of the most modern small cities in the country. The town has hundreds of new buildings, including a new fire station, city hall, and library, plus a new mall in the middle of the downtown business district.

Not all of Charles City's historic structures were destroyed, however. One of its landmarks is the downtown Charles Theater, built in 1935 in an art deco design with a facade of glittering gold lead and terra cotta. At one time hundreds of such theaters dotted the small towns of Iowa, but today only a handful remain intact. The town's Suspension Bridge is also a historic landmark, built in 1906 to connect the main part of the city with the county fairgrounds and the Chautauqua festivals held there. The single-span structure is over 200 feet in length, with a 4-foot-wide pedestrian walkway.

Charles City also boasts one of the largest county museums in Iowa, the **Floyd County Historical Museum.** The museum is housed in the former Salsbury Laboratory Building constructed in 1933 and contains over forty rooms of exhibits. Its best-known display is a complete original drugstore that operated on Charles City's main street from 1873 to 1961. The store was founded by German immigrant Edward Berg and was later owned by John Legel, Jr., who donated it to the historical society in 1961. Tour the store today and it's like stepping back a generation or more. The shelves are filled with patent medicines designed to cure every ailment known, plus items like cigar molds, chimneys for kerosene lamps, ink bottles, and cosmetics like 7 Sutherland Sisters Hair & Scalp Cleaner.

Elsewhere in the museum you can see a restored 1853 log cabin, displays of old-time vehicles and tools, and materials relating to the history of the county. The museum also contains the nation's most complete collection of information relating to the founders of the gasoline tractor industry, the Hart-Parr Company. The business was founded in Charles City and produced the first successful gasoline tractor in

125

1901. Another display contains information about Carrie Chapman Catt, a Charles City native and early leader in the women's suffrage movement.

The Floyd County Historical Museum is located at 500 Gilbert Street and is open year-round Monday through Friday from 10:00 A.M. to 4:00 P.M. During the months of May through September, the museum is also open on Saturday and Sunday from 1:00 to 4:30 P.M. Admission is $2 for adults, $1 for ages 12 to 18, and 25 cents for ages 5 to 12. For more information, call (515) 228–1099.

Off the Beaten Path in Western Iowa

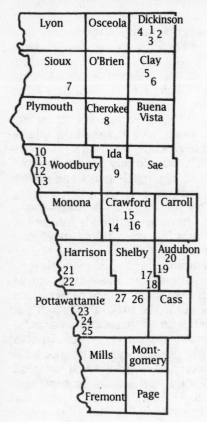

1. Arnolds Park
2. *The Queen II*
3. University of Okoboji
4. Cayler Prairie
5. Hannah Marie Country Inn
6. Inkpaduta Canoe Trail
7. Orange City
8. Sanford Museum and Planetarium
9. Aviation Expo
10. Sergeant Floyd Welcome Center/River Museum
11. Sioux City Public Museum
12. Woodbury County Courthouse
13. Loess Hills
14. Simon E. Dow House
15. W. A. McHenry House
16. Donna Reed Festival for the Performing Arts
17. Danish Windmill
18. Bedstemor's House
19. Little Mermaid
20. Albert the Bull
21. DeSoto National Wildlife Refuge
22. Bertrand Museum
23. General Dodge House
24. Ruth Anne Dodge Memorial
25. Squirrel Cage Jail
26. Iowa's Antique City
27. Victorian Bed and Breakfast Inn

Western Iowa

Dickinson County

This scenic county has been a popular recreation spot ever since the railroad first opened the area to development in the early 1880s. Known as the Iowa Great Lakes Region, Dickinson County contains thirteen lakes, the largest being Big Spirit Lake and West Lake Okoboji. Here you'll find some of the best swimming, boating, fishing, camping, and golfing in the state, in a beautiful setting surrounded by sparkling water. Once you visit, you'll realize why midwesterners have been flocking to the area for over a hundred years.

Many of the charms of Dickinson County are best discovered on your own—antiques stores, lovely parks and nature areas, fine restaurants, and quiet walks by the water. On your tour be sure to schedule time for a visit to **Arnolds Park,** an amusement park that has been attracting visitors to the area since 1915. Within the past few years it has undergone $1.25 million in improvements, a renovation designed to update the park without destroying its old-fashioned flavor.

A highlight of any visit to Arnolds Park is a ride on one of the country's few remaining wooden roller coasters, the Coaster. The ride made its debut in the park in 1929 and has thrilled thousands of children (and adults) with its clackety-clack ride and stomach-churning maneuvers. When Arnolds Park was being restored, a top priority was saving the local landmark. The Coaster was completely dismantled, cleaned, repainted, and refurbished, and new side rails, bearings, cars, and brakes were installed. Today it is once again the park's featured attraction, drawing roller-coaster connoisseurs from across the country.

The Coaster isn't the park's only asset. Twenty-five new rides and attractions, gift shops, restaurants, picnic areas, and sandy beaches will tempt you into relaxing. The park's new Majestic Pavilion revives another lake tradition, that of dancing and fine musical performances by local and touring artists.

The Coaster, Arnolds Park

Arnolds Park is located on the south side of West Lake Okoboji off Highway 71. General admission is $3.50, and the park is open from Memorial Day through Labor Day. Sunday through Friday it opens at 11:00 A.M., and on Saturday, at 10:00 A.M. For more information, call (712) 332–7781.

Another attraction in the area with a long history is *The Queen II,* a faithful reproduction of the 1884 *Queen* that plied the waters of the Iowa Great Lakes for eighty-nine years. Local volunteers are responsible for her existence, working both to help raise money for the boat and to help with her construction. More than half of the boat's $350,000 cost was raised through auctions, bake sales, and door-to-door solicitations. In 1986 the *Queen II* was officially launched, with Iowa Governor Terry Branstad commissioning her as the "Flagship of the Iowa Navy."

Today the *Queen II* offers five daily excursions from Memorial Day through Labor Day on West Lake Okoboji. The cruises last for ninety minutes, with the captain providing a narrative of the history and attractions of the region. Rates are $6 for adults and $4 for children. Call (712) 332–5159 for more information.

History buffs will want to further explore the area's colorful past. Indians first settled near the lakes after being pushed westward by settlers, but by the mid-1800s the area was attracting more and more white people. The tension between the two groups eventually led in 1857 to the infamous Spirit Lake Massacre, in which forty settlers were killed by a band of warriors led by the Dakotah Sioux chief Inkpaduta. The murders sparked an Indian uprising that echoed through Minnesota and the Dakota Territory.

You can learn more about the history of the area at several sites in Dickinson County. The Gardner Cabin in the town of Arnolds Park was the only dwelling left standing after the massacre and is now a museum as well as the last resting place for the victims of the tragedy. The cabin is also the site of the Spirit Lake Massacre Monument, erected by the state in 1895 in memory of those who had lost their lives. The Dickinson County Museum in Spirit Lake contains additional information on the massacre, plus displays on the steamboat and railroad eras and other historical items from the Iowa

Great lakes area. In Okoboji, visit the Higgins Museum, the largest banking and bank note museum in the Midwest.

No description of the Iowa Great Lakes Region would be complete without mention of the **University of Okoboji.** Its campus is one of the largest in the world, stretching from the northern tip of Big Spirit Lake to south of Milford. As you walk through its campus you'll see many signs of a strong school spirit: thousands of bumper stickers, sweatshirts, and pennants proudly bearing the university's name and hundreds of trash barrels that read HELP KEEP YOUR CAMPUS CLEAN. Prospective students will be relieved to learn, however, that the administration of the University of Okoboji believes that standard academic pursuits like books and lectures are unnecessary to true learning. Instead, its students major in roller-coaster engineering at Arnolds Park, culinary arts at local restaurants, and human anatomy at local beaches.

The school was founded over a dozen years ago, when Herman Richter (director of student affairs), his brother Emil (administrative dean), and Roger Stolley (director of admissions) ordered T-shirts emblazoned with the university's logo to wear at local sporting events. Before long, the joke had spawned a local—and then a national—phenomenon. Today there are U of O alumni chapters all over the country, made up of former visitors to the Great Lakes Region. The school has its own radio station, KUOO, and even established an endowment fund that is used to support community projects. Each year many local events are sponsored by the school, including a homecoming weekend, rugby tournament, and world tennis classic. Its football team, the Phantoms, is undefeated despite one of the most grueling schedules in college football: It's not unusual for the Phantoms to play the University of Iowa at 1:00 P.M., Nebraska at 4:00, and Notre Dame at 8:00. At each game, all the tickets sold are for Row A, Seats 1 and 2 on the 50-yard line, with proceeds going for a dome over West Lake Okoboji. University officials concede that the school's amazing record is helped by the fact that no other teams ever show up to play but contend that their team's excellence is so intimidating that other schools know they could never win.

Even if you can't get tickets for the U of O football games, you'll still enjoy your time as a student at the University of

Okoboji. The tuition is low, the classes are easy, and each year everyone graduates at the top of the class.

One final spot should be on your list of Dickinson County attractions. **Cayler Prairie** is a 160-acre tract of virgin prairie located west of Big Spirit Lake and is one of the largest remaining areas of prairie in the state. It is both a State Botanical Preserve and a National Historic Landmark, and it will give you a chance to see a little of Iowa's once-vast grasslands as they appeared more than a century ago. As you walk through its waist-high grasses, it's easy to imagine how it must have seemed to the early pioneers. Here you will find more than 250 types of grasses and wild flowers. Blooming begins in April with delicate pasque flowers and ends in October with brilliant blue gentians. Other wild flowers can be found in bloom throughout the summer, with the height of color to be seen in early August. The prairie is also home to badgers, fox, jackrabbits, meadowlarks, partridge, and the rare upland sandpiper.

Cayler Prairie is located 6 miles west of Big Spirit Lake off Highway 9. A parking lot is provided along the country road on the southwest side of the prairie. Visitors are welcome during daylight hours but are urged to read the regulation signs before entering the prairie. The picking or digging of plants is forbidden because of the rarity of many of the prairie's species.

Clay County

While on a tour of Clay County, pay a visit to **Hannah Marie Country Inn** near Spencer, a "country Victorian" farmhouse that offers overnight accommodations for visitors as well as elegant afternoon teas and luncheons. Mary Nichols operates the inn while her husband and son run the adjacent 200-acre corn and soybean farm. Mary is a retired home-economics teacher who named their place *Hannah Marie* after her mother, and the three guest bedrooms bear the names of her three aunts. Her warm touch is evident throughout the house, from the fat, handmade pillows in the antique rockers to the lace curtains at the windows.

The two-story frame farmhouse offers a comfortable place

to relax and unwind. Each room comes with a complimentary parasol and walking stick for jaunts around the farm, and the Nichols' library offers a variety of books if you'd rather just curl up with a good novel in the porch swing. In the morning you'll be served a hearty breakfast that concludes with a rich dessert, such as raspberry strudel drizzled with chocolate sauce and topped with cinnamon whipped cream.

The Hannah Marie Country Inn is also well known for its luncheons and afternoon teas, each organized around a different theme. Mary offers a regular round of ethnic teas (including Danish, Irish, and English), as well as Tea with the Mad Hatter (a favorite with young girls) and special events such as a Rosemaling Tea, during which a folk artist explains and demonstrates her craft.

The Hannah Marie Country Inn is located off Highway 71 south of Spencer. It is open from May through December, and room rates are $50 to $60. Prices for the teas and luncheons are inexpensive to moderate. For reservations, call (712) 262–1286 or (712) 332–7719.

Another attraction that begins in Spencer is the **Inkpaduta Canoe Trail** on the Little Sioux River. The trail winds for 134 miles from Spencer south to the town of Smithland in Woodbury County. The Little Sioux is the largest interior stream of the Missouri River watershed in Iowa and has a sand, mud, and gravel bottom and high banks along most of its scenic course. The river current is quite slow, which makes for excellent fishing as well as canoeing.

The trail is named for the Sioux Indian who led the Spirit Lake Massacre. Inkpaduta and his followers were never caught after the raids, which ignited anti-Indian sentiments and raised fears throughout the Midwest.

As you travel the canoe trail, you can focus on a happier topic by keeping your eyes on the lookout for river otter. Once the most prevalent mammal in North America, unregulated hunting and trapping and habitat destruction decreased its numbers to the point of extinction in Iowa. In 1985 a program was started to reintroduce the river otter to the state. Iowa's native wild turkeys were trapped and traded for Louisiana otters. To date more than 170 otters have been released at the Little Sioux River near Peterson. If you're lucky enough to see one of these graceful creatures, you're asked to report the information to the office of a county conservation board along the trail. Many other animals can be seen along the river as well, including great blue herons, raccoons, beavers, muskrats, turtles and white-tailed deer.

The Inkpaduta Canoe Trail can be entered at various sites. For a brochure and map, write to the Clay County Conservation Board, 420 South Tenth Avenue SE, Spencer, 51301; or call (712) 262–2187. (Don't plan on using the trail in winter.)

Sioux County

Founded in 1870 by Dutch pioneers, the town of **Orange City** in Sioux County takes great pride in its ethnic heritage and offers a number of attractions. Here you can see a variety of Dutch architecture (including a drive-in bank housed in a windmill), hundreds of beautiful flower beds full of tulips in season, and stores selling traditional Dutch dolls, pottery, lace, baked goods, wooden shoes, and meats.

Each spring during the third weekend in May, Orange City becomes even more of a Little Holland during its annual Tulip Festival. One of its most popular attractions is the Volksparade, when hundreds of people take to the streets with their buckets and scrub brushes to make the way clean for the festival's queen. Then board the Wilhelmina or the Juliana, the town's two horse-drawn streetcars, to see the rest of the sights in town. The Dutch Street Organ will likely catch your attention—one of only two in the United States, the organ was built in Holland and plays melodies for the enjoyment of passersby. The Dutch Dozen is a musical and dance group that will also entertain you, and in the evening you can kick up your own heels in a street dance or attend a theater performance.

At any time of year you can visit the Century Home, a house built in 1900 by Orange City's first mayor and decorated with furnishings that might have belonged to a typical Orange City family at the turn of the century. Included within are a pump organ handmade in 1903, a silver tea service that belonged to the home's original owner, and a clock brought from the Netherlands by the founder of Orange City. One of the upstairs rooms is filled with memorabilia from former tulip queens. The home is located at Albany Avenue and Fourth Street NE and is open throughout the year from 8:30 A.M. to 4:30 P.M. Monday through Friday.

At the Old Mill at the entrance to the Vogel Paint and Wax Company you can learn more about the Dutch influence in Orange City. The site contains three different types of windmills and an office building designed after a Dutch *stadshuis* (city hall). The Old Mill itself has displays on how wind power can be used for a variety of purposes, while the living quarters show life as it was generations ago. Some of the furnishings were brought from Holland, and others came from local pioneers. The Old Mill is open Monday through Friday from 9:00 A.M. to 5:00 P.M., May through October.

And before you leave Orange City, stop by the Royal Dutch Bakery at 221 Central Avenue NE. There you can buy such treats as almond patties, St. Nick cookies, Dutch rusks, apple rolls, and Wilhelmina Peppermints imported from Holland.

For more information on attractions in the Orange City area, call the town's chamber of commerce at (712) 737–4510.

Cherokee County

The town of Cherokee in central Cherokee County is the site of the **Sanford Museum and Planetarium,** the first museum in the state to be accredited by the American Association of Museums. The facility was donated to the town by a local couple in memory of their son, Tiel Sanford, and was officially opened to the public in 1951. Since then, more than three-quarters of a million people have viewed its displays.

Permanent exhibits at the Sanford deal with a variety of subjects relating to this region of the country and its past. Rocks, minerals, and fossil and animal specimens help explain the environment of the region, and there are also displays on the native American tribes who once lived in the area.

The planetarium was built in 1950 and was the first such facility in Iowa. Planetarium shows are given on the last Sunday of each month at 2:00 P.M. Groups can also schedule shows by appointment.

The Sanford Museum and Planetarium is located at 117 East Willow Street in Cherokee. Its hours are from 9:00 A.M. to

5:00 P.M. Monday through Friday and from noon to 5:00 P.M. on Saturday and Sunday. Admission is free. For more information, call (712) 225–3922.

Before you leave Cherokee County, you might want to pay a visit to one of its natural landmarks located about 2 miles south of the city on Highway 59. Pilot Rock is an enormous boulder of red Sioux quartzite about 160 feet in circumference and 20 feet high. It was left behind when the last continental glacier receded and offers a panoramic view of the surrounding landscape. During pioneer days, Pilot Rock served as an important landmark for travelers.

Ida County

Visit the town of Ida Grove in central Ida County and you'll be surprised to see castlelike structures interspersed with typical midwestern architecture. The man largely responsible for the eclectic mixture is Byron Godbersen, founder and owner of Midwest Industries in Ida Grove, a manufacturer of farm and marine equipment. Godbersen has a taste for Spanish and Mediterranean architecture and has constructed many buildings here that are a fanciful mixture of styles, from the fortresslike Midwest Hangar and Convention Hall to his own home complete with moat, watchtower, and drawbridge. Other projects include a Skate Palace now operated by the American Legion and a half-scale model of the famous ship, the H.M.S. *Bounty.* A driving tour of Ida Grove is a must for any visitor to the town.

Godbersen is also the driving force behind the **Aviation Expo,** billed as the "World's Most Unique Aviation Event." Anyone who attends is likely to come away convinced of the claim's truth. The event is hosted by Byron Originals Model Aircraft Company, a Godbersen enterprise that manufactures one-fifth-scale remote-controlled airplanes and jets. The five-day expo is the country's largest gathering of radio-controlled aircraft fans and features aerobatic and air-show performers, modeling forums, manufacturer's exhibits, and a wide variety of aviation-related events.

The highlight each day is "Striking Back," a World War II battle reenactment staged at a one-fifth-scale mountain range complete with a railroad, oil refinery, miniature ocean, and warships. Some fifty people are needed to coordinate the extraordinary event, which has enough explosions and buzzing planes to satisfy anyone who grew up with a passion for playing soldiers.

The Aviation Expo is held each August in Ida Grove, and admission is $5 for adults. For more information, write to Byron Originals Expo, Inc., P.O. Box 253, Ida Grove, 51445; or call (712) 364–3167.

Woodbury County

At one time Sioux City, the county seat of Woodbury County, had a wild and wooly reputation that was known throughout the country. The city was a major river port and became the center of a booming stockyard and meat-packing industry. Sioux City has another claim to fame: The nation's two most famous advice columnists, Abigail Van Buren ("Dear Abby") and Ann Landers, were born here in 1918. The two are identical twins who were christened with the names Pauline Esther Friedman and Esther Pauline Friedman.

On a tour of the area, you're likely to come across several references to another famous figure in Sioux City history, Sergeant Charles Floyd. Floyd was a young man living in Kentucky when he was recruited by his relative William Clark to be part of the famous Lewis and Clark Expedition that was sent to explore the vast reaches of the newly acquired Louisiana Purchase in 1804. Floyd kept a journal of his adventures, a diary full of entries that describe both the important and the ordinary happenings of the expedition: "Capt. Clark and 10 of his men and myself went to Mahas creek a fishen and caut 300 and 17 fish of difernt kinds," is a typical entry.

The young man's great adventure came to an end, however, when he became ill as the party was traveling through what is now the Sioux City area. He died August 20, 1804, the only casualty of the two-year Lewis and Clark Expedition and the first American soldier to lose his life west of the Mississippi. Today a tall obelisk, the Sergeant Floyd Monument, marks his grave site on a high bluff overlooking the Mississippi River. The monument became the country's first National Historic Landmark in 1960 and is located off Highway 75.

The young soldier is also remembered at the **Sergeant Floyd Welcome Center/River Museum** in Sioux City. This is an interstate highway welcome center housed aboard an original 1932 Army Corps of Engineers inspection vessel, named in honor of Sergeant Floyd. From 1933 to 1975 the boat did towing, survey, and inspection work on the Missouri River, and in 1983 it was permanently dry-docked to serve as a combined welcome center and river museum. On the main deck you'll find tourist information and on the second deck an Upper Missouri River history museum. The displays include the largest collection of scale-model Missouri River steamboats in the Midwest.

The Sergeant Floyd Welcome Center/River Museum is located off Interstate 29 at Exit 149. It is open year-round, from 9:00 A.M. to 6:00 P.M. daily.

Another spot worth a visit is the **Sioux City Public Museum,** housed in one of the most spectacular homes ever built in the city. Its original owner was John Peirce, an early Sioux City realtor and developer who lost his fortune soon after building the house in the early 1890s. The house is a Romanesque mansion of Sioux quartzite with twenty-three rooms filled with stylish paneling and ornately carved woodwork.

On the first floor of the museum you'll find exhibits on Sioux City history, the Civil War, and life on the frontier. The second floor has displays on natural history, fossils, and minerals, while the third floor is devoted to an extensive native American collection. On display are various Indian artifacts, including articles of clothing and beautiful quill and bead work. Most items are from the Plains and Woodland tribes that once inhabited this area.

The Sioux City Public Museum is located at 2901 Jackson Street. Its hours are Monday through Saturday from 9:00 A.M. to 5:00 P.M. and on Sunday from 2:00 to 5:00 P.M. Admission is free. For more information, call (712) 279–6174.

The **Woodbury County Courthouse** should be on your list of attractions if you're interested in architecture. Unique among Iowa courthouses, the building was designed by architects who had worked with the famed Louis Sullivan in Chicago. The largest public building in the country to be executed in the Prairie school style, the courthouse reflects the aesthetics of Sullivan. Inside are decorations of terra cotta, stained glass, polished tile, and mosaic inlay, plus rotunda murals by Chicago artist John W. Norton. Though the design was called "unusual and extreme" by critics of the day, today it's considered one of the state's most significant architectural landmarks.

The Woodbury County Courthouse is located at Seventh and Douglas streets in Sioux City. It is open Monday through Friday from 8:00 A.M. to 5:00 P.M. Call (712) 279–6505 for more information.

No description of western Iowa would be complete without mention of the **Loess Hills.** The hills begin just north of Sioux City and stretch in a narrow band south to the Missouri state line and are formed from deposits of windblown silt—a unique geological phenomenon found only in Iowa and in the Kansu Province of northern China. In places they look like a miniature mountain range rising out of the Iowa plains, soft hills covered with a mixture of prairie and woodland plants. They were formed after the retreat of the last glaciers and since then have been eroded by wind and rain into the beautiful ridges and valleys visible today.

The Loess Hills contain an amazingly diverse ecosystem of plant and animal life that has long fascinated scientists. Dense forests line the sheltered areas of the hills, while the more exposed slopes are almost desertlike. Unfortunately, many parts of the hills are in danger because of erosion, development, and overgrazing. The state is hoping to establish a protected state forest in the area, but until then you can enjoy the hills at a number of public areas along the Iowa border: Stone Park in Sioux City, the Loess Hills Wildlife Area in Monona County, various county roads in Monona and Harrison counties, Desoto National Wildlife Refuge near Missouri Valley, and Waubonsie State Park in Fremont County are all good viewing spots.

Cornelia F. Mutel's book *Fragile Giants* will give you more information on exploring the Loess Hills and their delicate ecology. The book is available from the University of Iowa Press, University of Iowa, Iowa City, 52242.

Crawford County

Two historic homes in Crawford County are worth making an effort to see. One is the **Simon E. Dow House** in Dow City, a lovely home located high on a hill with a commanding view of the surrounding countryside. Its builder, Simon Dow, was traveling through Iowa on his way to California in 1855 when he decided to cut his journey short and remain here because he liked the area so much. Later he became a prominent cattleman, and in 1874 he built a substantial red-brick house that became the nucleus of a settlement called Dow City. At a time when the average house cost $2,000, Dow spent $11,000 for his home.

The Dow House is unique in that its floor plan is the same on all three floors. All the walls are three bricks wide to keep the home warm in the winter and cool in the summer, and ornamented keystones and carved roses are centered over the first- and second-floor doors. Today the home has been restored to its original state and will give you an interesting introduction to the lifestyle of a prominent, upper-middle-class citizen of the nineteenth century.

The Simon E. Dow House is located south of Highway 30 at the end of Prince Street in Dow City. It is open from May through October, from 1:00 to 5:00 P.M. Tuesday through Sunday. Admission is $1 for adults and 50 cents for children. For more information, call (712) 674–3734 or (712) 263–2693.

Travel north on Highway 30 for 7 miles and you'll come to Denison, site of the **W. A. McHenry House.** This beautiful Victorian home was built in 1885 by Denison pioneer William A. McHenry. With six fireplaces and fourteen rooms (including a ballroom), the home was for many years a showplace for the area. Today it has been restored and contains a variety of historical artifacts.

The W. A. McHenry House is located at 1428 First Avenue North in Denison. It is open Wednesday, Thursday, and Sunday from 1:00 to 4:00 P.M. from Memorial Day through Labor Day. Admission is $1 for adults and 50 cents for children. For more information, call (712) 263–3806.

The town of Denison also takes pride in its status as the birthplace of everyone's favorite mom, actress Donna Reed.

Reed was raised on a farm near Denison and completed her schooling here. After graduation she left Iowa to become an actress, starring in "The Donna Reed Show" and more than thirty movies, including *From Here to Eternity,* for which she won an Oscar for best supporting actress (the Oscar is now on display at the W. A. McHenry House). Reed returned often to Denison until her death in 1986, remaining in contact with her family and friends in the area.

In honor of the famous actress, each June Denison hosts the **Donna Reed Festival for the Performing Arts.** The festival draws an impressive list of professionals: In years past participants have included Debbie Reynolds, Shelley Fabrares, Nanette Fabray, and Bonnie Franklin, plus nationally known writers, directors, and producers. Workshops are held on various topics relating to musical theater, television, writing, acting, and directing, and large assemblies and small group discussions are offered. At the conclusion of the festival, a picnic is held for the visiting artists, workshop participants, and the general public.

The Donna Reed Festival for the Performing Arts is held each year in Denison on the first weekend in June. For more information, call (712) 263–5621.

Audubon and Shelby Counties

On the border between these two counties you'll find the quiet villages of Elk Horn and Kimballton, home to the largest rural Danish settlement in the United States. In these communities you can still hear Danish spoken on the street, and the telephone book is filled with good Danish names like Christensen, Overgaard, Johansen, Madsen, and Andersen. Danish immigrants settled the area in the late nineteenth century, and their descendants have worked hard to preserve their unique heritage.

Your first stop on a visit to the area should be the towering **Danish Windmill** in Elk Horn. The landmark brings to mind the bumper sticker that says, YOU CAN TELL A DANE, BUT YOU CAN'T TELL HIM MUCH. If that weren't the case, it's doubtful the historic mill would ever have left its home in Norre Snede, in the Danish province of Jutland. It was during the height of the farm crisis in the mid-1970s that local resident Harvey Sornson came up with the idea of finding a Danish windmill to bring to the area. Many people thought the idea was crazy, but their skepticism gradually gave way to Sornson's persistence. A mill was located in Denmark, and an emergency town meeting in Elk Horn resulted in $30,000 being pledged to the project in just a few days. The 1848 structure was then laboriously dismantled and brought over piece by piece to Iowa. When it arrived it still had ocean salt on its timbers, and eighty-seven-year-old Peder K. Pedersen, who had left Denmark at the age of twenty-one and never returned, tasted the salt of a distant sea and cried.

Many townspeople worked together to reassemble the jigsaw puzzle of the dismantled mill, which was rebuilt in 1976. The total cost of the project eventually came to $100,000, an amount raised through fund-raising projects and contributions from all over the country. Today the windmill stands some 60 feet high, with four 30-foot wings that catch the wind, turn the gears, and grind locally grown grain. The base of the mill houses a welcome center with extensive tourist information, and the adjacent Danish Mill Gift Shop offers stone-ground flour and a wide selection of Scandinavian gifts and foods.

The Danish Windmill is located on the main street in Elk Horn and is open every day except Sunday morning (hours vary slightly depending on the season). Tours of the mill are available for $1.50 for adults and 50 cents for children. For more information, call (712) 764–7472.

Another Elk Horn attraction that owes its existence to the town's volunteer spirit is **Bedstemor's House,** meaning "grandmother's house." More than a hundred volunteers have donated time, materials, and furnishings to restore the 1908 home. Inside you'll find a glimpse of the life of a Danish immigrant family at the turn of the century. (To furnish the home, volunteers used a 1908 Sears Roebuck catalog as their guide.)

Bedstemor's House is located 3 blocks north and 1 block west of the Danish Windmill in Elk Horn, at 2105 College Street. It is open daily (call for hours), and admission is $1.50 for adults and 50 cents for children. For more information, call (712) 764–8932.

Danish Windmill

At the Danish Bakery at 4234 Main Street, you can sample such ethnic treats as *smorrebrod, rullepolse, kringle,* and *kransakage* (the bakery's fame is so widespread that it even offers a shipping service for homesick Danes across the country). The Elk Horn Grocery and Locker offers additional ethnic foods and meats, while the Danish Inn serves Danish as well as American specialties. Another popular stop for overnight visitors is The Traveling Companion, a bed-and-breakfast in a 1909 home owned by Karolyn and Duane Ortgies. Each guest room is named after a fairy tale by Hans Christian Andersen. Call (712) 764–8932 for more information.

In future years travelers will find an additional attraction on their visits to Elk Horn. Work is in progress on a new $12 million National Danish Immigrant Museum, which will chronicle the history of the Danes who came to this country seeking a better life. In 1983 a nationwide search was conducted to select a location for the new museum, and Elk Horn was chosen over numerous other Danish settlements because of its strong town spirit and commitment to the project.

Two miles north of Elk Horn you'll find its sister village of Kimballton, also an enclave of Danish-American culture. The town's pride and joy is the **Little Mermaid,** a statue modeled after the famous landmark in Copenhagen's harbor (the Little Mermaid, of course, is the immortal character from the fairy tale by Hans Christian Andersen). Kimballton's little mermaid is the focal point of the town's Little Mermaid Park on Main Street. Nearby is the Mermaid Gift Shop featuring many imported gift items.

While touring Kimballton you may also want to visit the General Store Museum, where you can see antique toys, vintage machinery, and examples of the skill of the Danish immigrant mason Nels Bennedsen. The building was constructed in 1910 and was used as a barbershop until 1940. Its hours are from 1:00 to 5:00 P.M. Monday through Saturday, from May through October.

A good time to visit this area is during its two annual Danish festivals. Tivoli Fest is held each year on Memorial Day weekend. Julefest (the town's Christmas festival) is held the weekend after Thanksgiving and celebrates the season in true Danish style. Whenever you visit, you're likely to leave these friendly communities with an appreciation for their Danish heritage and with plans to return again. For more information on attractions in Elk Horn and Kimballton, call the Danish Windmill Corporation at (712) 764–7472.

Northeast of Iowa's Danish villages you'll find the town of Audubon, proud owner of **Albert the Bull.** He's a difficult critter to miss, as he weighs forty-five tons and towers thirty feet in the air. Albert was built in 1964 as a tribute to the local beef industry and was named in honor of Albert A. Kruse, a local banker and promoter of the cattle business (one hopes that Mr. Kruse was flattered, not insulted, by the recognition). The bull was built by the Audubon Jaycees, who first constructed a rectangular I-beam structure with quarter-inch steel rods to give Albert his portly shape. Then concrete was applied to the frame, and sixty-five gallons of red and white paint turned Albert into a member of the Hereford breed. The result? Well, let's just say that Albert is a prince among cattle—and that's no bull. Albert the Bull (also known as the World's Largest Bull) can be seen south of Audubon off Highway 71.

You can recover from the excitement of seeing Albert at Nathaniel Hamlin Park, located 1 mile south of Audubon on Highway 71. The park features a nature area with ponds, wildlife, and wild flowers, plus a museum, farm with eighteen historic windmills, dairy barn, little red schoolhouse, and an antique farm implement museum.

Harrison County

Harrison County contains some of the most varied and beautiful scenery in the state of Iowa: lush farmland, gently rolling foothills, and the fragile loveliness of the Loess Hills. The county is also known as an apple-producing area. The fruit was first planted here before 1880, and today Harrison County has more acreage in apples than any other county in Iowa. The orchards, many of which line the county roads, are located near the towns of Missouri Valley, Mondamin, Pisgah, and Woodbine. Several orchards have facilities for picking your own apples, and orchard tours are also available.

Apples are available for sale from mid-August to the end of the season. For more information, call the Harrison County Development Corporation at (712) 644-3081.

Near the town of Missouri Valley in Harrison County you'll find one of the state's major wildlife areas, the **DeSoto National Wildlife Refuge,** located 5 miles west of Interstate 29. The refuge lies on the wide plain formed by prehistoric flooding and shifting of the Missouri River. Each spring and fall since the end of the last ice age, spectacular flights of ducks and geese have marked the changing seasons along this traditional waterfowl flyway. During a typical year some 200,000 snow and blue geese use the refuge as a resting and feeding area during their fall migration between their arctic nesting grounds and their Gulf Coast wintering areas. Peak populations of 125,000 or more ducks, mostly mallards, are common in the refuge during the fall migration. Other birds commonly seen in the area include bald eagles, warblers, gulls, pheasants, and various shorebirds.

Bird life is not the only attraction at the refuge. Deer, raccoons, coyotes, opossum, beaver, muskrat, and mink make their home here and can often be seen by patient observers. During the spring and summer, the refuge is open for fishing, picnicking, mushroom and berry picking, hiking, and boating. Twelve miles of all-weather roads meander through the refuge, and during the fall a special interpretive brochure is available to guide visitors and explain the annual migration.

The visitor center at the refuge should definitely be part of your visit to Harrison County. In addition to natural-history displays, viewing galleries, wildlife films, and special programs, the center is also the site of the **Bertrand Museum,** a facility housing some 200,000 artifacts recovered from the steamboat *Bertrand,* a vessel that sank with all its cargo in the treacherous Missouri River in 1865.

The wreck of the *Bertrand* mirrors that of many steamers, 400 of which sank in the Missouri during the nineteenth century. The boat was a mountain packet stern-wheeler designed for the shallow, narrow rivers of the West. It was built to carry supplies that would eventually find their way to the gold miners of the Montana Territory and was said to be loaded with 35,000 pounds of mercury, $4,000 in gold, and 5,000 gallons of whiskey—a fortune worth $300,000 or more. Luck was not with the steamer, however, for on her first trip upriver she hit a snag and sank in 12 feet of water. The passengers and crew escaped unharmed, but the bulk of the cargo had to be abandoned. By the time a full-scale salvage operation could be mounted, the boat was irretrievable.

Over the years many treasure hunters searched unsuccessfully for the *Bertrand* and her costly cargo. With time, the Missouri changed its course, leaving the boat in a low-lying field under 25 to 30 feet of silt and clay. It wasn't until 1967 that the wreck was located after an extensive search by treasure hunters Sam Corbino and Jesse Pursell. Unfortunately for them, the cargo didn't contain the rumored riches, though it did contain bounty of another sort: some 10,000 cubic feet of hand tools, clothes, foodstuffs, furnishings, munitions, and personal effects, a virtual time capsule of nineteenth-century life. What was even more remarkable was that most of the cargo was in an excellent state of preservation, though the boat itself had to be returned to its resting spot once the artifacts were removed.

Visit the Bertrand Museum today and you can view many of those items, a collection that provides a fascinating look at a vanished time. More than the story of the *Bertrand* is revealed here: The saga of the western expansion unfolds through the boat's artifacts and other exhibits depicting the history and wildlife of the Missouri River Basin.

The Bertrand Museum, located in the DeSoto National Wildlife Refuge Visitor Center, is open from 9:00 A.M. to 4:30 P.M. daily, except for New Year's Day, Easter, Thanksgiving, and Christmas. Additional interpretive displays can be seen at the *Bertrand* excavation site 3 miles south of the visitor center. Admission to the refuge is $2 per vehicle. For more information, call (712) 642–4121.

More of the history of the area can be viewed at the Harrison County Historical Museum, located 3 miles northeast of Missouri Valley on Highway 30. Included in the museum are ten buildings, including an 1853 log cabin, 1868 school, mill, harness shop, fur museum, broom factory, and chapel. The museum also serves as one of Iowa's official welcome centers and offers a large selection of brochures and other visitor information.

Pottawattamie County

Pottawattamie County is an area rich in history. Its major city, Council Bluffs, marks the spot where the explorers Lewis and Clark held council with the chiefs of the Otoe and Missouri Indian tribes in 1804. The city later became a major stopover point on the Mormon Trail, and it was here that Brigham Young was elected as president of the Mormon Church in 1847. By the mid-1800s Council Bluffs had become a wild and lawless town, a place where "gambling and sin of almost every description flourished." The Ocean Wave Saloon was one of the most notorious sporting houses in the entire West until it burned to the ground during a violent thunderstorm (some held that it had been struck by lightning, while others believed it was the wrathful hand of God). Henry DeLong, a former regular customer of the establishment who had mended his ways, bought the property and gave it to the Methodist Church with the provision that it be used forever after as a church site. The Broadway Methodist Church now stands on the property, and it's most likely the only church in the country with a plaque on the front commemorating a saloon.

Council Bluffs' most famous and influential citizen was General Grenville M. Dodge, a man who has been called the greatest railroad builder of all time. Born in the East, Dodge first saw Council Bluffs while making a railroad survey and was so captivated that he made the city his home in 1853. In 1859 he met Abraham Lincoln and the two developed a strong friendship. After Lincoln became president he appointed Dodge as the chief engineer of the first transcontinental railroad. During the Civil War Dodge served with distinction in a number of positions and was responsible for creating the first military spy system. After the war he was elected to Congress without campaigning and later became an advisor to Presidents Grant, McKinley, Roosevelt, and Taft, as well as a business leader in Council Bluffs and the East.

Today you can visit the **General Dodge House** to learn more about the life and times of this remarkable man. The home was built in 1869 and was designed by William Boyington, who was also the architect for Terrace Hill in Des Moines (p. 82). The Second Empire–style mansion stands on a high hillside overlooking the Missouri Valley and contains lavish furnishings, parquet floors, cherry, walnut, and butternut woodwork, and a number of "modern" conveniences quite unusual for the period. Today it has been restored to the opulence of the general's day and is open for tours.

The General Dodge House is located at 605 Third Street in Council Bluffs and is open from 10:00 A.M. to 5:00 P.M. Tuesday through Saturday and from 1:00 to 5:00 on Sunday. It is closed during the month of January, and the last tour begins each day at 4:00 P.M. Admission is $2.50 for adults and $1.00 for children. For more information, call (712) 322–2406.

General Dodge's wife, Ruth Anne, added a bit of color to the city and is commemorated by the **Ruth Anne Dodge Memorial.** On the three nights preceding her death in 1916, Mrs. Dodge had a dream of being on a rocky shore and, through a mist, seeing a boat approach. In the prow was a beautiful young woman whom Mrs. Dodge thought to be an angel. The woman carried a small bowl under one arm and extended the other arm to Mrs. Dodge in an invitation to drink of the water flowing from the vessel. Twice Mrs. Dodge refused the angel, but on the third night she accepted the invitation to drink—and died the next day.

Dodge's two daughters later commissioned Daniel Chester French, who also sculpted the *Lincoln Memorial* in Washington, to construct a statue of the angel in memory of their mother. Though the daughters were reportedly disappointed with the finished work, the monument is now considered to be one of French's finest works. Today you can see the graceful angel, cast in solid bronze, in Fairview Cemetery. As in Mrs. Dodge's dream, the heroic-sized statue holds a vessel of water and beckons with her hand.

The Ruth Anne Dodge Memorial, also known as the *Angel of Death,* is located in Fairview Cemetery at Lafayette and North Second streets.

Another historic monument in Council Bluffs is the **Squirrel Cage Jail,** once considered the ultimate in prison facilities. The unique design was patented in 1881 by two Indiana men with the idea of providing "maximum security with minimum jailer attention." Also called a "lazy Susan" jail, the cell block consists of a three-story drum surrounded by a metal cage. Each of the three decks contains ten pie-shaped cells, with only one opening on each level of the drum. To enter a cell, the jailer would turn the central drum so that a cell doorway was lined up with the cage opening—like a squirrel cage. It may seem dehumanizing today, but in 1885 when it was opened, the jail was considered an improvement over the damp, unsanitary quarters prisoners had been kept in previously.

Though it remained in use up until the 1960s, the jail was declared a fire trap in 1969 because only three prisoners could be released at one time during an emergency. It was later in danger of being destroyed when the Pottawattamie County Historical Society launched a heroic effort to save it. The jail was named to the National Register of Historic Places in 1972 and is now owned and operated as a museum by the Historical Society.

On a tour of the Squirrel Cage Jail, you'll also see the jailer's quarters and office and a room filled with prison memorabilia. Today the site is one of only two "lazy Susan" jails still standing in this country.

The Squirrel Cage Jail is located at 226 Pearl Street in Council Bluffs. It is open Wednesday through Saturday from 11:00 A.M. to 5:00 P.M. and on Sunday from 1:00 to 5:00 P.M. The last tour begins at 4:00 P.M. Admission is $2 for adults and $1 for children. The jail is closed January, February, and all legal holidays. For more information, call (712) 323-2509.

Before you leave Council Bluffs you might also want to visit one of its other attractions, including Bluffs Run (its greyhound racetrack), the Stempel Bird Collection on display in the Pottawattamie Court House, and the Transportation Museum in Dodge Park. Another popular attraction in the city is the Pathfinder Dinner Train, a refurbished passenger train offering a fine menu of evening meals.

For more information on attractions in the Council Bluffs area, contact its convention and visitors bureau at (712) 325-1000 or (800) 798-TOUR.

The small town of Walnut in northeastern Pottawattamie County calls itself **Iowa's Antique City,** and after paying a visit to its downtown, you're likely to agree. There are nearly twenty antiques stores here, making Walnut one of the best havens for nostalgia buffs in the state. Between the independently owned shops in town and four large antiques malls, more than ninety antiques dealers sell their wares here. From antique brass beds to ice-cream parlor stools and vintage dollhouses, you're likely to find an eclectic mixture of treasures on a visit to Walnut.

Though Walnut has had several antiques dealers in town for the past decade, within the past five years the number of stores has greatly increased. The town's location right off Interstate 80 helps, as does its old-fashioned downtown. Many of the storefronts here look virtually the same as they did more than sixty years ago. And because the overhead costs are lower here than in a larger city, you can often find lower prices on Walnut antiques.

Another attraction in Walnut is the old Opera House, which is in the process of being restored. In addition to a performing arts theater, the structure will contain a country music museum and the Iowa Country Music Hall of Fame.

For more information on Iowa's Antique City, contact Eldon and Marilyn Ranney, owners of The Victorian Rose antiques store, at (712) 784–3588.

Travel 6 miles west to the town of Avoca and you'll find a pleasant place to recover from your shopping expedition. This peaceful little town draws its name from a place mentioned in Thomas Moore's Irish melody "The Meeting of the Waters." Each year Avoca hosts the National Old-Time Country Music Contest and the Pottawattamie County Fair, and the town also maintains a beautiful park with a restored one-room schoolhouse dating back to 1858.

Another highlight of Avoca is the **Victorian Bed and Breakfast Inn,** a bright yellow Queen Anne Victorian home built by one of Avoca's leading businessmen in 1904. The inn is owned by Gene and Jan Kuehn, who met at a dancing school, married shortly thereafter, and "have been waltzing ever since," according to Jan.

Inside, the home has been elegantly and lovingly restored. All of the woodwork is of southern yellow pine, and the dining room and parlor are graced with finely detailed columns that set off large and airy windows. The four guest rooms are decorated with antique oak and walnut furnishings and lace curtains, and each of the two shared baths come with a refinished antique tub (in addition to a new tile shower, for those who prefer convenience to atmosphere).

The Victorian Bed and Breakfast Inn is located at 425 Walnut Street in Avoca. Rooms rent for $50, which includes a hearty breakfast. Guests can also arrange to have a home-cooked lunch or dinner at the inn. For reservations call (712) 343–6336 or (800) 397–3914.

Index

Index

Dubuque County, 2
Dyersville, 6

E
Eagle Point Park and Nature Center, 42
Edel Blacksmith Shop, 105
Effigy Mounds National Monument, 12
El Charro Mexican Restaurant, 36
Eldon, 61
Elkader, 9
Elk Horn, 141
Ellston, 98
Emmet County, 118
Emmetsburg, 117
Ertl Toy Factory, 6
Esterville, 118
Esterville Winter Sports Festival, 118

F
Fairfield, 60
FantaSuite Hotel, 35
Farm Arts and Artisans Festival, 105
Farmington, 69
Fayette County, 18
Fenelon Place Elevator, 5
Festina, 16
Field of Dreams, baseball diamond, 7
Fish Farm Mounds, 12
Floyd County, 125
Floyd County Historical Museum, 125
Fort Atkinson State Preserve, 16
Fort Dodge, 113
Fort Madison, 71
Fort Museum, 114
Fremont County, 139
Frontier Days, 114
Future Birthplace of Captain James T. Kirk, 54

G
Garrison, 51
General Dodge House, 148

Index

About the Author

Lori Erickson is a freelance writer and native Iowan who grew up on a farm near Decorah. She holds degrees from Luther College and the University of Iowa, and her articles and essays have appeared in dozens of regional and national magazines and newspapers. She is the author of three collections of Iowa ghost stories published by Quixote Press and is a member of the Midwest Travel Writers Association.

Lori lives with her husband, Bob, and young son, Owen, in Iowa City.

Other Books of Interest from The Globe Pequot Press

Off the Beaten Path series

Colorado • Florida • Georgia • Illinois
Indiana • Maryland • Minnesota • New Jersey
New York • North Carolina • Southern California
Tennessee • Virginia • Wisconsin

Recommended Country Inns series

New England • Mid-Atlantic and Chesapeake Region
The South • The Midwest • Rocky Mountain Region
Arizona, New Mexico, and Texas

Don't be puzzled about Iowa.

Learn about your state and others with the enjoyable and educational 100-piece puzzles in the Austin-Pierce "Puzzlin' State" puzzle series.